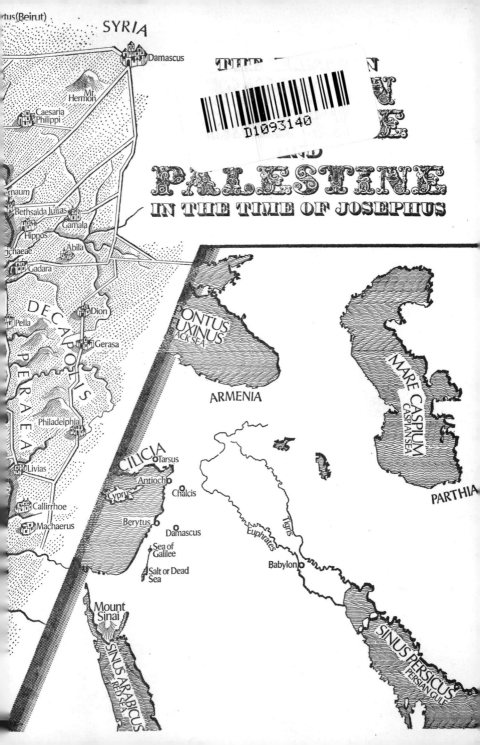

PEOPLE FROM THE PAST—No. 14
EDITED BY EGON LARSEN

FLAVIUS JOSEPHUS
The Jew who rendered unto Caesar

FLAVIUS JOSEPHUS

The Jew
who rendered unto Caesar

———

OLIVER COBURN

LONDON - DENNIS DOBSON

First published in Great Britain in 1972
by Dobson Books Ltd.
80 Kensington Church Street, London, W.8

ISBN 0 234 77690 0

PRINTED IN GREAT BRITAIN BY
WILLMER BROTHERS LIMITED, BIRKENHEAD

Contents

Illustrations

On Wednesday the Jews came home

It was Wednesday June 7th, 1967. Dawn began
to clear the dark of the crooked streets of old
Jerusalem, and with it came the artillery. It
struck at the Jordanian Arab Legion defending
the Mount of Olives, where Christ had predicted
the destruction of Jerusalem and ascended into
Heaven; and it struck at Gethsemane, where He
had prayed after the Last Supper.

At 8.30 a.m. Israeli paratroopers dropped near
Mount Scopus, where Titus and his Romans had
camped before they conquered Jerusalem. Tanks
and infantrymen completed the encirclement of
the Old City, and the soldiers fought their way
in through the gates much as David and his men
had done three thousand years before. They
fought down the narrow streets, along the drain-
age ditches bridged by gravestones from the
Jewish cemetery on Mount Sion. A platoon
assaulted the Dung Gate—so called because in
years past the city's sewage had been dumped
there—but was blocked by Jordanian machine-
guns. The crouched soldiers could see the Dome
of the Rock, a holy shrine to Islam, only a few
feet from the cherished stones that remained of
the ancient Jewish Temple—the Wailing Wall . . .

Israeli tanks from the Jordanian side rolled
through St. Stephen's Gate in the east of the Old
City. To their right was a sign saying that the

Virgin Mary had been born there. Israeli foot-soldiers fanned out towards the Wailing Wall. Jordanian machine-gunners shot at them from the gate-house protecting the Dome of the Rock —shellfire badly damaged the church of St. Anne, built by the Crusaders 800 years ago.

By midmorning Arab resistance in the Old City was broken.

Already weeping Jews, citizen soldiers, were making their first pilgrimage to the Wailing Wall. They stood and prayed, they knelt and prayed, they caressed and kissed the stones, their faces drawn with the emotion of two thousand years of flight and persecution. Above the heads of the soldiers, helmets in their hands, the Wall seemed again a Temple, small green plants clinging to the ancient crevices as Jews had clung to the hope of returning here.

'We have taken the City of God,' said the Chief Rabbi of the armed forces. 'We are entering the messianic era for our people. But I promise to the Christian world that we will take care of the holy places of all religions here.'

There is no holier place for the Jew than the Wall. Hundreds now stood before the age-old stones, dampening them with their tears as the angels are reputed to have done when Titus destroyed the Temple. 'We have waited one thousand eight hundred and ninety seven years for this moment' cried a paratrooper, beating his campaign hat in the dust.

(*Associated Press*, describing the climax of the Six-Day War)

PROLOGUE:
IF I FORGET THEE,
O JERUSALEM

'The City of God,' said the Rabbi. How true this sounds, when you think that Jerusalem is central to two world religions, Judaism and Christianity; while to a third, Islam, it has a special importance as a Holy City. No wonder, then, that it has been looked on, through the greater part of 3000 years, as the most important city in Palestine, ancestral home of the Jewish people, who pioneered the belief that there is only one God.

So Palestine is a Holy Land indeed. Yet this beautiful small country (about the size of Wales) has often been turned into a battleground, fought over with the most unholy savagery. Certainly its geographical position in the cockpit of the Middle East—a vital strategic and commercial bridge between the valleys of the Nile and the Euphrates, between Africa and Asia—has not made for a peaceful existence. But many of the repeated struggles for power involving Palestine have been inflamed by religion, as in the Crusades, when Christian kings and popes tried to wrench the country away from Muslim rule. The Ottoman Turks conquered it in 1517, and for four centuries it remained within the Ottoman Empire, stagnating socially and economically, more or less isolated from history.

Then in December 1917, at the height of the First World War, the British general, Allenby, liberated Palestine from the Turks. A month before this the British government had issued the famous Balfour Declaration—so-called after the British foreign minister—viewing with favour 'the establishment of a National Home in Palestine for the Jewish people' without prejudice to 'the civil and religious rights of existing non-Jewish communities in Palestine.'

Few can have realised at the time quite how completely these two parts of the Declaration contradicted each other, especially as promises of independence, after liberation from the Turks, had also been made to Arab leaders in the area, who assumed this would extend to Palestine. Till then the small number of Jewish settlers had lived at peace with the Palestinian Arabs, but the great Zionist dream was for more than a 'national home'—it was for a Jewish state. Not only would ancient glories be revived, age-old longings fulfilled. More crucially, Jews would have a place of their own, a haven from the persecution to which, scattered all over the world, they were constantly subjected.

From 1920 onwards the British government, administering the country under a League of Nations mandate, tried vainly to hold the balance. Their difficulties were immensely magnified when the Nazis produced their 'final solution' to the Jewish problem—the policy of mass murder which led to the death of six million Jews during the Second World War. The stream of immigrants became a flood, threatening to swamp the native inhabitants of the Twice Promised Land. Arabs throughout the Middle East reacted with new violence to what they saw as a wholly European problem being settled at their expense; while Europe's Jews grew increasingly desperate, their longing for Palestine more and more intense.

In 1948 Britain gave up the Mandate amidst anarchy and savage fighting. When the dust of battle had settled, Jerusalem was divided between Transjordan (now Jordan) and the new independent state of Israel. Transjordan held the Old City, which contained the Christian Holy Places, the Muslims' superb Mosque of Omar—or 'Dome of the Rock' and the Wailing Wall, part of the western wall of the ancient Jewish Temple, for the loss of which the Jews had always 'wailed'. The Mosque, which stands on the site of the Temple, is where Muslims believe that Mahomet ascended to Heaven.

Jerusalem's uneasy partition lasted until the Six-Day War of June 1967, when a victorious Israel captured the Old City and took possession of the whole of their people's historic capital. 'If I forget thee, O Jerusalem,' they had cried of old in the captivity of Babylon, 'let my right hand forget her cunning.' Now the task of the strong right hand was carried out. There was tremendous jubilation, balanced by the implacable bitterness of the defeated Arabs, of the whole Arab world. But at this thrilling moment in time it was understandable that few Jews should take account of that or feel any pity for thousands more uprooted refugees. The Temple area was in Jewish hands once more for the first time since 70 A.D.

In that year their glorious shrine had been destroyed in the sack of Jerusalem by Roman legions under Titus, son of the Emperor Vespasian. The Arch of Titus still stands today in Rome, commemorating the Temple's destruction.

There was one Jew who unwillingly witnessed the disaster from enemy lines. His name was Joseph Ben Matthias. Formerly a leader in the great Jewish rebellion against the Roman Empire, he had gone over to the Romans, and as Flavius Josephus, a Roman citizen, he wrote the history of the rebellion, which he called *The Jewish War*. A protégé of Vespasian and his family, he spent the rest of his life as a writer, and completed three more works. By far the longest is a history of the Jews from the Creation onwards, *The Jewish Antiquities*. The other two are a defence of the Jews against their enemies, commonly called *Against Apion* —Apion was a prominent 'anti-Semite' of that time; and a very unbalanced *Life*, almost entirely devoted to the part Josephus played in the war. (The word 'anti-Semite' is used in its unscientific modern sense of anti-Jewish.)

All his works have a propaganda purpose, and they are often unreliable. But we are extremely lucky that they survived, for their historical value is immense, giving a fascinating detailed picture of the much-disputed Holy Land at a key point in the story of mankind's development. Born just after the crucifixion of Jesus of Nazareth, Josephus saw the beginnings of the new Jewish sect which came to be known as the Christians. He was also an expert witness of the clash between two ancient civilisations, and took an important part in its tragic climax.

The Roman Empire was direct heir to the culture of the Greek city states, which came to its finest flowering in fifth-century Athens and had spread over most of the known world through the conquests of Alexander the Great. With this Graeco-Roman civilisation the Jews could never fully come to terms. Long centuries of tradition kept them a people apart from the 'Gentiles', the other nations.

CHAPTER I

A PEOPLE APART

Somewhere around 2000 B.C. the patriarch Abraham, by modern standards a nomadic sheikh, came to the land of Canaan, west of the river Jordan, promised to him in a special covenant with Jahweh, his God. In the Genesis story Abraham's grandson Jacob gained Jahweh's blessing after a wrestling bout, and was afterwards called Israel, which means 'he who strives with God'. His son Joseph became a powerful man in Egypt, and his descendants, 'the Children of Israel', remained there for many generations. They 'multiplied', and because of their numbers became unpopular with the rest of Egypt's population—until their Exodus under Moses, celebrated ever afterwards in the Feast of Passover. Moses led them into the wilderness, and the covenant was renewed on Mount Sinai, where he received the Ten Commandments, foundation of Jewish ethics and law: the first time in recorded history that divine worship was explicitly linked with human morality.

At the beginning of the twelfth century B.C. the 'twelve tribes' of the Children of Israel entered Canaan, where they gradually conquered all the native tribes, except for the Philistines who had settled on the coast. Greek sailors called the whole country by the name they were familiar with; hence the name Palestine, derived from the name of the Israelites' defeated enemy. For in the end the Philistines *were* defeated, in the great days of the Prophet Samuel, of Saul and David. A golden age started in the reigns of King David and his son Solomon (tenth century). Solomon's wealth and wisdom were equally celebrated, and he built the magnificent Temple at Jerusalem. But he filled it with heathen shrines and started the process of assimilation to Israel's neighbours, through alliances and political marriages, thus watering down the stern faith and morality of the twelve tribes.

After his death their fortunes declined. His heirs quarrelled, and ten of the tribes formed a northern kingdom, Israel, with its capital at Samaria, while a southern kingdom called Judah, made up of the other two tribes, had its capital at Jerusalem. Samaria in later times gave its name to the Samaritans, the neighbours of the Jews, half related but usually hostile.

In both kingdoms the tradition linking morality with religion and politics was upheld by the prophets, who opposed even kings if kings disobeyed God's laws. They were statesmen and social reformers, their task was not foretelling the future (as later prophets did) but proclaiming God's message. Part of the message was a theme which occurs again and again in Jewish history, and was often used by Josephus: that sin inevitably brings retribution on the state.

In 722 the northern kingdom fell to Assyria; a century and a half later Judah succumbed to Babylon, and the ruling families were carried off into exile, where they languished for fifty years. 'How can I sing the Lord's songs in a strange land?' they lamented, and 'If I forget thee, O Jerusalem, let my right hand forget her cunning.' So when Cyrus, King of Persia, took Babylon in 538 and allowed all Jews who wished to return to Palestine—although many families had settled down and preferred to stay in their new country—50,000 trailed across the desert to reach the land of their fathers. Twenty years after their return the Temple was restored and rededicated.

For the next three and a half centuries the Jews inhabited an area of about eighty miles round Jerusalem, living in comparative tranquillity with enough independence to maintain and extend their ancestral traditions.

During the Exile Jews had taken to meeting on the Sabbath to read from their sacred books or listen to a religious leader's reflections on these books. Ezra, one of the last great prophets, revived these Sabbath meetings, which developed into the synagogue (the Greek word for an assembly). This has remained an essential feature of Judaism, and of Christianity and Islam too, for church and mosque are based on the synagogue. Ezra began the training of teachers—called Scribes—to interpret and explain the *Torah*, his revised code of Jewish laws; and the local religious leaders also administered justice. So the synagogue became both school and court, part of the life of every Jewish community anywhere.

The people were ruled by a High Priest, who acted as local governor *and* religious leader: power was thus concentrated in men supposed to be directly representative of God. Josephus claimed that he was himself coining a new word 'theocracy' (rule by God) to describe the Jewish form of government. The High Priests came from the aristocratic families, and it is not surprising that wealth and power often corrupted them.

Meanwhile Alexander the Great had carried the Greek language and Greek ideas to Egypt and far into Asia. Barbarians lived in villages, the Greeks thought, whereas Hellenic culture was based on the city state. He founded many fine cities, such as Alexandria, and so did his successors.

His campaigns and the wars between his successors brought an increase in the numbers of Jews 'in the Dispersion' (outside Palestine): some fled, others were enslaved and later freed. Alexandria in particular became the home of a very large Jewish community, and the Pentateuch (the five books of the Law) were translated into Greek. This was very important both for preserving the faith and for making converts.

The pattern for Alexandria was typical of the many Hellenised cities which grew up then and later. Jewish tradition was safeguarded by the organisation of Jews in independent communities, with synagogues in every city that had a community. It was a society rather like the modern Freemasons, which gave its members special advantages as well as duties. The main distinctive features were the belief in one God; an advanced social morality; keeping the Sabbath and the Festivals; circumcision; and obedience to a great many detailed laws laid down by Moses. Some of these related to morals, others—for instance those on diet—were health rules. For the Jews they were hallowed by sacred tradition, and it was important to observe them all.

Circumcision was perhaps originally a health rule too. Many ancient peoples had practised it, and at the time of David the Jews talked of 'the uncircumcised Philistines' because every other people they knew did it. But with the others it was a puberty rite of admission to the tribe, whereas for the Jews it had turned into an infant rite of admission to the People of God, a sign of their covenant with God, instituted by Abraham. So while the Gentiles discarded it, the Jews stood out by retaining circumcision as an essential part of their religion.

A great many men and women outside Palestine sympathised with the Jewish faith but did not become full Jews: the Jews called them 'God-fearers'. They too, like Jews everywhere, sent money to the Temple at Jerusalem, which was another thing resented by their neighbours in the Greek cities. These Jews were more loyal to distant Jerusalem than to their own city; and how they stuck together, turning those noses up at their fellow citizens!

But Jews were not always exclusive: even in Palestine quite a number of them, especially the rich and aristocratic families, were themselves tempted by the advantages of the Greek way of life. This led to the first great clash, in the second century B.C., between Judaism and Hellenistic civilisation. It also brought the Jewish people back into world history.

The Syrian king Antiochus, encouraged by some leading Jews, tried to turn Jerusalem into a Greek city called Antioch, and eventually, faced by guerilla warfare, determined to stamp out the Jewish religion. He sent out an order prohibiting Sabbath observance, the festivals, circumcision; had swine sacrificed on Jewish altars, the books of the Law burnt, and the Temple profaned by the worship within it of heathen gods.

Many Jews submitted, but others remained loyal to the Torah, including one group who refused to defend themselves on the Sabbath and were all massacred. They are among the first non-violent martyrs in history. But the rebellion proper started when Syrian troops came to a village to make the inhabitants bow down to the pagan gods. Old Mattathias the Priest killed first a Jew who was about to obey, then the king's commissioner appointed to carry out the royal decree. Then he fled to the hills with his five sons.

One of these was the national hero Judas 'Maccabaeus' (the Hammer), who united the mass of the people in their defence of the Torah and the Temple. Just as 'the might of the Gentile' (the army of Senacherib the Assyrian) had once 'melted away in the glance of the Lord', so those who kept His commandments could expect similar miraculous aid, however invincible the enemy might look.

Judas and his brothers live on in Jewish tradition as the Maccabees, because of Judas's nickname, although Josephus always refers to them as the Hasmonaeans after Hashmon, father of Mattathias. He proudly claimed descent from them on his mother's side, since his great-great-grandfather married the daughter of Jonathan, one of the brothers. He started his long prologue to *The Jewish War* with an account of the persecution by Antiochus, justifiably. For the Jews who defied the might of Rome were acting very much in the spirit of the Maccabees.

After defeating two Syrian forces and keeping a third at bay, Judas took Jerusalem, where in 164 B.C. he solemnly cleansed and rededicated the Temple. The occasion is still celebrated every year at Hannukah (dedication), the joyful eight-day Feast of Lights. This is the only Jewish festival not prescribed in the Bible, which shows its immense significance: thanksgiving for a Holy War. In a modern context, it is worth noting that Judas wreaked terrible vengeance on the Syrian population in other cities who had attacked their Jewish communities.

Judas died in battle (in 160), but his successors gradually won complete independence from Syria, till they were Kings as well as High Priests. But the purity of

Hannukah had been lost. Brutal, lax in morals, unpopular with their own people, they launched wars of conquest, with armies of foreign mercenaries, and extended the Jewish territory to something like the area it reached under Solomon, including Galilee to the north, Peraea to the east and Idumaea (to-day's Negev) to the South. The Idumaeans were now forced to adopt Judaism, including circumcision. One of their chieftains was left as governor; his son Antipater later took revenge by ruling over his country's conquerors.

After a peaceful nine-year reign by the only queen in the Jewish state's history, civil war developed between her two sons, one supported by Antipater. This gave a pretext for the first Roman invasion of the country.

Founded in 509 B.C., the Republic of Rome had been pushing its power ever further. By the first century B.C. the Romans felt the whole civilised word was under their sway. They were tempted by the wealth of the East to further conquests, but here they came up against the kingdom of Parthia—in the north west of the modern Persia—which remained a dangerous enemy.

Pompey, the Roman general in the East, quickly mastered all Asia up to the Euphrates, and made Syria a Roman province. In 63 B.C., despite fierce resistance from one of the Jewish factions, he captured Jerusalem after besieging the Temple, and left the shrewd Antipater, who had backed him, as governor of the country now called Judaea, part of the province of Syria. 12,000 Jews had been killed, thousands more were sent to Rome as slaves. Many of these were later freed, which led to a large Jewish community there. Pompey behaved 'correctly', taking none of the Temple treasure, but it was a deep shock to Jewish pride that he had penetrated into the inner sanctum, the Holy of Holies, which only the High Priest might enter. It proved symbolic, too: never again was Judaea to be completely independent of Rome.

Coin of Queen Alexandra

CHAPTER 2

HEROD THE GREAT

The Roman Republic was governed by a Senate of patricians (noble families) with two annually elected magistrates called consuls. The vast majority of the population were plebeians, the common people, with very little influence over events. Further still down the social scale, there were large numbers of slaves, usually captured in foreign wars; in 73 B.C. the Republic had been seriously threatened by a massive slave revolt.

Even more dangerous, the Senate had become virtually powerless against army commanders, and a succession of civil wars took place between rival generals: Marius and Sulla, Pompey and Caesar, then Brutus and Cassius against Antony and Octavian (Caesar's great-nephew and adopted son). In 31 B.C., when he had defeated his former ally, Antony, and the Egyptian Queen, Cleopatra, at Actium, Octavian was at last ruler of the whole Roman world.

So began the Roman Empire. Octavian had the title of Augustus conferred on him, and although he restored some of the Republican forms, it was clear that he intended to keep full control of the government. He governed with efficiency and ruthlessness, softened by tact. A world weary of bloodshed, where the masses had never known real freedom, was simply grateful for peace restored.

To curb the power of the patricians, Augustus extended

the function of the 'knights', and formed an imperial civil service from them. Many were freedmen (former slaves), who came to have an increasing influence under his successors.

The Emperor also set out to link religion with the state. It was an age of ferment, and mystery religions flourished, while the old Graeco-Roman deities made very little appeal intellectually or emotionally. To offset this and increase the solemnity of his own position, Augustus had Caesar, his adoptive father, declared a God. He called himself Caesar Augustus, and the name Caesar gradually became a title for all Emperors. They and Rome were to be thought of as eternal, like the *Pax Romana* (Roman Peace), the supreme benefit which Augustus was conferring. In 9 B.C. he dedicated his great Altar of Peace, which can still be seen today.

For his successors, peace was precarious, often disturbed by palace intrigues and also by generals and mutinous armies. But for the peoples of the Empire it lasted almost exactly a century—with a few interruptions, mainly on the frontiers.

Augustus died in 14 A.D., after reigning for forty-four years, and was at once declared a god. In Rome the succession passed peacefully to Tiberius, his obvious heir; but the German legions tried to impose their own commander, Germanicus, Tiberius's nephew, as the new Emperor. Germanicus remained loyal, however, and Tiberius ruled till his death in 37. Germanicus had died, leaving a son, Gaius, nicknamed 'Caligula' (little boot) by his father's troops.

At the end of Augustus's reign there were about twenty five provinces in the Empire, all paying tribute to Rome. But in some countries, instead of provinces, Augustus set up what today we should call puppet kingdoms. It saved

Roman man-power, and helped to appease nationalism. The kingdoms in the East also acted as buffer states between the Empire and the Parthians.

One of these kings was in a unique position: Herod of Judaea.

After Pompey's defeat and death, Antipater had gone over to Caesar. He helped him in Egypt, and was rewarded by being made 'procurator' of Judaea. By a decree of Caesar's the Jews had to pay an annual tribute; but they were exempted from military service, allowed to judge cases in their own courts and live according to their own laws. When Caesar was murdered, on the Ides of March 44, the Jews mourned him sincerely.

A year later, Antipater was poisoned by an enemy. His son Herod soon showed all his father's skill in backing the winning Roman general. A friend of Antony's, legend has it that he was the only man who refused to succumb to Cleopatra's charms. While Antony and Octavian-Augustus were still allies, they made the 33-year-old Herod king of the Jews (in 40). But it took three years of civil war, including another siege and capture of the Temple, before he established himself in Jerusalem with Roman help.

Augustus recognised an able ruler likely to control a troublesome nation and provide safe lines of communication between Egypt and Syria. With one brief interval, Herod kept the Emperor's good-will all his life; Augustus showed special favour to his sons, who were educated at Rome. Herod's title in the Empire was 'Friend and Ally of the Roman People'.

His policy had three main objectives: to keep down Jewish nationalism, break down the rigid barriers between Jews and the Graeco-Roman world, and promote the welfare and honour of Jews everywhere—for he was a generous patron of the communities in the Dispersion.

He also tried hard to satisfy the demands of the Jewish religion, but in Judaea itself many hated and distrusted him: for his readiness to compromise with pagan culture and politics; as an alien Idumaean, who was barely a Jew at all; and for his equally generous patronage of non-Jewish cities. They disapproved of his founding such magnificent new cities as Sebaste, formerly Samaria, and Caesarea (on the coast below Mount Carmel), and giving them temples with shrines to Roman deities, to Augustus and to Rome.

To suppress nationalism, he established a police state, with spies and informers to forestall any conspirators. He kept a standing army, largely composed of non-Jewish mercenaries, and set up a chain of forts at strategic points, notably one called the Antonia in Jerusalem, and the two on the Dead Sea, Masada and Machaerus. The great rock of Masada had first been built on by Jonathan the Hasmonaean, but Herod turned it into an impregnable fortress. His original aim was partly to foil Cleopatra's designs on his kingdom, but also (Josephus writes) 'for fear of the multitude of the Jews, lest they depose him and restore their former kings to the government'.

He was ruthless in crushing 'bandits', and many of these bandits were what we should now call guerillas. But this policy was evidently effective; for his reign lasted thirty six years, and except at the end, when he was ill and half-mad, no serious rebellion disturbed the peace. The country was mainly agricultural, with most of its wealth based on corn, wine, olives, and fruit; fishing, flocks and herds. The bulk of the population were small-holders, who in good years would export their surplus grain, olive oil, and fruit. Under Herod they could till their land undisturbed. Peace, order, safe roads made for increasing trade and prosperity.

Moreover, the climax of the King's public works was to the glory of God and His people: the magnificent rebuilding and expansion of the Temple, badly damaged in successive sieges. Work started in 19 B.C., and within a year and a half services could be held in the new inner shrine; the vast enclosure took another eight years. The most majestic religious centre in the world, it was built, significantly, in the Greek tradition with its porticoes and Corinthian columns. The gilded pinnacles gleaming in the sunlight summed up Herod's aspirations to greatness. For, in the words of the historian Stewart Perowne, 'All that the Hellenism of the day could furnish of rare beauty and massive strength was dedicated to the Holy One of Israel.'

How did the recognized Jewish leaders react to such aspirations? These leaders, who made up the Sanhedrin—or Supreme Court, came from the two main religious sects, the Sadducees and the Pharisees. They were only a small minority of the population, a few thousand at most.

The Sadducees had supported the Hasmonaean kings, and so at first opposed Herod, who purged the Sanhedrin to reduce their power. But later they may have become reconciled to his rule. They provided the High Priests, and were very much a Temple 'party'. Big land-owners, rich and aristocratic, they benefited by the security of Herod's reign and even accepted his readiness to fall in with Greek ideas. They had their prestige and authority increased by the glories of the new Temple. Herod's powerful friend Agrippa, the Emperor's son-in-law and right-hand man, had honoured it during a state visit to Jerusalem, by sacrificing a hundred oxen. (Animal sacrifice was still a prominent feature of Temple worship.)

The Sadducees are generally thought to have been called

after Zadok, chief priest in King Solomon's time. They recognised only the written law, whereas the Pharisees had developed out of the Scribes, teachers of the Law from Ezra's day. They brought in many new laws which could be applied in a changed society, and they aimed to provide rules and guidance for every part of daily life. Politically, they were more radical and more opposed to pagan influences. But it does not work exactly to make them out 'a party of the left' as against the 'right-wing' Sadducees, because they were divided themselves, between two leading Rabbis (teachers and interpreters of the Law): Shammai and Hillel.

Shammai was harsh and intolerant, shunning all contact with Gentiles, ready to approve of violence in defence of the Torah. Hillel (75 B.C.–10 A.D.) believed in the brotherhood of man, encouraged converts to Judaism, and hoped that Jews would act like leaven in the world, exerting influence by moral force. Gentle and compassionate, he told his followers to 'seek peace and pursue it'.

For the most part his views prevailed over Shammai's, though both were recorded as precedents for later use. It was convenient for Herod that such a distinguished religious leader as Hillel should have a concern for social welfare combined with a code for living at peace within the established order. At one point Josephus says that the main part of Herod's magnanimity 'was extended to the promotion of piety', which suggests that he showed favour to Hillel and the Pharisees of that school.

There was a third important sect, the Essenes. They tried to preserve the full purity of the Torah by retiring from the sinful world and leading strict ascetic lives in isolated communities. We hear that Herod honoured Menahem, a leading Essene. These communities were not designed

Flavius Josephus as pictured in the famous Whiston edition of his works (1737).

Nero

Augustus

Titus

Vespasian

Four Roman Emperors

for political action, so they presented no danger to the King.

Apart from the militant wing of the Pharisees, what threatened his power most seriously were the feuds and intrigues at court, which may have partly caused his mental illness and certainly aggravated it. To make his dynasty more secure, he had married a Hasmonaean princess, who was one of his ten wives. He loved her, but suspected her of conspiring against him, and in 29 B.C. had her executed, only to feel bitter remorse on discovering afterwards that she was innocent.

In his private life he never recovered from this. Josephus describes in far too much detail the family plots and counter-plots and the terrible crimes committed by the old King, pain-racked and demented, during the last ten years of his life. He had three of his sons executed, although, strangely enough, he was kind to the children of the first two, and took personal charge of their upbringing. One of these children was the future King Agrippa, named after Herod's Roman friend.

Herod's reputation as a monster of cruelty, however, is largely due to the story in Matthew's Gospel of the Massacre of the Innocents at Bethlehem—which Josephus does not mention. Matthew and Luke differ on several points concerning the birth of Jesus, and for history Luke is probably the more trustworthy of the two. If he is right, Jesus was born in 6 A.D., the date of the Roman census, when Herod was already ten years dead. The reference might conceivably be to his son, Herod Antipas, ruler of Galilee. Otherwise, unless Matthew is right, the origins of the story are wholly mysterious.

In 4 B.C., a band of youths cut down a golden eagle which the King had placed above the great door of the

29

Temple. They claimed this was against the Law of Moses, and two leading Pharisees incited them to the act. Forty of them were caught and arrested with the two Pharisees, and Herod, though dying, lay on a couch to hear the case himself. They were convicted of sacrilege and burnt at the stake.

In the old King's fourth and last will he divided his kingdom between three surviving sons and a sister. After his death the situation soon became chaotic. Archelaus, the chief heir, failed to stop riots at the Passover, then set off for Rome to plead his cause with Augustus, because his brother Antipas was disputing the will. Meanwhile a Roman official from Syria occupied Herod's palace at Jerusalem, triggering off a rebellion all over the country, and two 'brigand chiefs' gained a brief control. But Varus, the Syrian governor, quickly crushed the rebellion, killing thousands of Jews; 2000 of the ringleaders were crucified. The 'War of Varus' remained a bitter memory to rank with the tyranny of Antiochus and Pompey's capture of Jerusalem.

Augustus, deciding between the claims of Herod's three sons, also heard a deputation of fifty Jewish notables from Jerusalem, supported by 8000 Jewish residents in Rome, who wanted him to remove all kings. The request is surprising: they delivered tirades against both Herod and Archelaus, but could they have expected Roman rule to be gentler?

The account by Josephus, incidentally, seems to have produced a reminiscence in Luke's Gospel: the parable of the Pounds, where a nobleman goes off into a far country to obtain a kingdom, but 'his citizens hated him, and sent an embassy after him, saying: "We do not want this man to reign over us." '

Augustus eventually decided to partition the country, leaving Archelaus with most of his father's territory, while

Antipas received Peraea and most of Galilee, and Philip a small region in the north adjoining Syria. Archelaus proved oppressive and brutal, and was denounced in 6 A.D. by both Jews and Samaritans, in rare combination. A ruler as unpopular as this was no use to Augustus, who recalled him and banished him to a town in Gaul. So what the deputation had asked for ten years before, now took place: Judaea became once more part of the Roman province of Syria. It is not clear why Augustus did not abolish the kingdom at Herod's death; perhaps because till then it had worked so well, giving him a trouble-free country in a very sensitive part of the Empire.

Both in *The Jewish War* and in *Antiquities* Josephus gives an immense amount of space to Herod. Some of his sources were hostile to Herod, but in the main he follows the idealised picture by Herod's court historian, so that on balance the bias is favourable. Making allowance for this, we can still accept that, for all his faults and final madness, the king presented in Josephus's pages deserved to come down to history as Herod the Great: for the splendour of his Temple, but more important, because he kept Rome at a distance. Judaea paid no tribute, saw no Roman officials or tax-collectors. Co-existence with Rome was made possible for the Jews largely because of the friendship between Herod and Augustus. With that factor removed, a collision course was set.

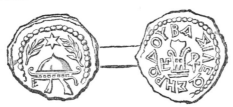

Coin of Herod the Great

CHAPTER 3

THE ROMANS MOVE IN

In the British Empire, at least during its final period, colonial administrators saw it as their mission to train the native peoples for eventual independence. This idea would have seemed absurd to the Roman Emperors, who had no thought of bringing into being new independent states. The provinces and puppet kingdoms were encouraged to adopt Roman culture, but the spread of citizenship was very limited. Roman citizens in the early Empire (which covered about a million and a quarter square miles) were concentrated largely in Rome and northern Italy.

Economically, too, the advantages of the Roman Peace were balanced by an exploitation of the subject peoples. The population of the Empire may have been about sixty or seventy million, but censuses were irregular. Their sole purpose was to bring the tax-rolls up to date. All provincial residents paid a direct tax to the central government at Rome, and all provincial land was the property of the Roman state.

In Republican days the Romans had farmed out provinces to tax-collectors known as *publicani*, who notoriously took every chance to get rich quick. The apostle Matthew was one of these 'publicans', and the phrase 'publicans and sinners' bears witness to their low reputation. Tiberius expanded the imperial civil service established by Augustus.

so that government officials, often just as greedy and corrupt, took over some of the responsibility for bringing in
the money. The tax-collector and the Roman soldier were
everywhere the most obvious link between the provinces
and Rome.

In Tiberius's time there were twenty-five legions, most of
them with permanent stations on the frontiers—four in
Syria, for instance, and two in Egypt. There was no central
reserve, and when they were moved from one frontier to
another in a crisis, the first frontier was seriously weakened.
Auxiliaries were mostly drawn from outside Italy, and
served in the areas where they had enlisted.

The richer and more settled provinces were still controlled directly by the Senate, while provinces like Syria
which needed garrisons were governed by *legati* (legates)
of senatorial rank but directly responsible to the Emperor.
Some of the smaller provinces were entrusted to procurators, originally financial officials, who were knights. Egypt,
under a prefect, was a special case, for memories of Cleopatra were all too recent: with Antony her willing slave,
the power of Rome had looked in danger of shifting to
Egypt. Augustus, therefore, kept a jealous eye on the
country, so important strategically as Rome's granary. Senators and knights were not allowed to enter it without a
permit.

Rome had begun to acquire provinces in the third century
B.C. and went on doing so until the second century A.D.
When Virgil, greatest of Roman poets, wrote his national
epic, *The Aeneid*, he contrasted the ideal of the Roman
state, standing erect through 'old-time' morality and men,
with the softer arts of the Greeks. The Romans' arts should
be to rule the nations with imperial sway and impose the
code of peace, 'to spare the humble and subdue the proud'.

Many provincial cities had a flourishing life, and enjoyed considerable self-government. With a chronic shortage of man-power, Rome depended a good deal on the local ruling classes, who could be expected to act as a pro-Roman counterweight to nationalist feelings. It paid off to interfere as little as possible with social and cultural institutions, although the Roman provincial governor retained almost absolute power.

Though very different in many ways, the provinces were made more like each other by the influence of Greek civilisation, which the Romans themselves had increasingly absorbed. Without much exaggeration the Augustan poet Horace wrote of captured Greece 'taking victorious Rome captive'. Greek was a second language for educated people everywhere.

Within this Hellenistic civilisation the Jews of the Dispersion occupied a unique position. They had long been accepted in all spheres of Roman life. They became minor and even major officials under the Republic, and continued to hold such offices under the Empire. Rome was generally tolerant of other religions, so long as they did not become entangled with political opposition, and this tolerance was generally extended even to the Jews. Still, the success of any alien faith might be dangerous, so the Roman attitude to the Jews was not always clear and consistent.

Their neighbours were usually hostile, resenting Jewish loyalty to a different country (Judaea), their exclusive attitudes, and the privileges entrenched by Roman law. Jews wouldn't dine with Gentiles, didn't attend pagan festivals and ceremonies, or contribute to the expenses of local cults. They were allowed to have their own meeting-houses, to import special food, to refrain from work on the Sabbath and Holy Days. Resentment of Jewish privileges and social aloofness led to more and more tension in Hellenised cities such as Alexandria, where there were about a million Jews —the largest number of any city outside Judaea. It was no wonder that the rest of the population showed many of the features of modern antisemitism.

Besides, the Jews were always making converts. People were attracted by the security of Jewish family life, their enlightened social, hygienic, and moral standards, the higher status they gave to women. Nor were they always exclusive. One of the noblest Jews of his age was the Alexandrian scholar Philo, born about 25 B.C., who tried to reconcile Greek philosophy with Judaism, to blend Plato and Moses. It was a highly original attempt, for no Greek philosophers would have seen the Sinai revelation as a source of knowledge higher than reason, nor had they any idea of a single God like the very active, personal, righteous God of the Jewish scriptures. Philo identified the Word (the *Logos*) with the law divinely given to Moses—compare 'in the beginning was the Word' in John's Gospel. He accepted the Stoic view that 'no man is a slave by nature', and preached that 'love of man must triumph in us over hatred of the enemy'. Presenting the universalist side of Judaism and its most exalted ethics, he wanted to make it a religion which would appeal to Gentile hearts and minds.

The fact that the Jews encouraged converts rather worried Augustus and his successors. For all their efforts to check the trend, the birth-rate in Italy continued to decline. The Jews, on the other hand, were a prolific race, whose numbers were increased by the converts. There were probably six or seven millions in the early Roman Empire (with another million outside it in Babylonia and Parthia). They formed about ten per cent of the Empire's population, and at least twenty per cent in the east, where they were mainly concentrated. In Judaea itself there were about three and a half million Jews. With these immense numbers, they seemed capable of becoming an empire within the Empire.

The whole Jewish problem loomed larger for the Romans from 6 A.D. on, when they took over direct rule of Judaea, and discovered just how difficult to handle these people were.

This new part of the province of Syria was governed by a procurator directly responsible to the Emperor, and the procurators of Judaea were keenly aware of his supervision, which added to the pressures on them. The Legate of Syria could and did intervene in special cases.

The Jews in Judaea, however, retained a good deal of self-government. The Sanhedrin still acted as supreme court, though without the right of pronouncing the death sentence. The High Priest still collected the Temple tax and the tithes prescribed in the Torah, but he was the nominee of the procurator, who administered the Temple funds, a bitter pill for the Jews to swallow. Moreover, the Graeco-Syrian civil servants on the procurator's staff were as a rule extremely hostile to the Jews.

The seat of government was Herod's palace at Caesarea, but the procurator and his staff would stay at Jerusalem during Jewish festivals when crowds poured in and riots were likely. There was a permanent garrison at Herod's fortress, the Antonia, overlooking the Temple, and the sight of Roman soldiers was a continual source of irritation to the Jews. With their contempt for Jewish customs, the troops, rather than contributing to good order, produced much extra friction.

Imperial taxation was another heavy burden, for most of the population was already very poor, and a drought or similar crisis could ruin thousands of peasants. Many would fall into the hands of money-lenders and lose their holdings. The Judaeans now had to pay an annual contribution in corn and cattle—and the tribute in money, which was a special offence to Jewish pride, since it had to be paid in coin bearing the Emperor's effigy.

A generation later the enemies of Jesus of Nazareth tried to trap him by asking whether Jews should pay tribute. They were told: 'Render unto Caesar the things that are Caesar's, and to God the things that are God's'. The famous answer was skilfully loaded to embarrass his questioners. For the resources of the Holy Land were not Caesar's, and should not be given to a heathen lord; yet Roman coin was a symbol of the international trade from which the richer Jews benefited so much.

Introduction of the tribute was preceded by a census, which is mentioned by Josephus as well as Luke. After protests the High Priest persuaded the people to accept it, but in the same year (6 A.D.) it set off a revolt by Judas of Galilee, and Zadok, a Pharisee of the militant wing. They founded the Zealot movement, so-called because of its zeal for the Law. The Zealots proclaimed that paying tribute to the Romans was the beginning of slavery. Josephus, who detested them, presents them consistently as bandits who misled the nation. Although in *Antiquities* he refers to them as a 'fourth philosophical sect', he plays down their religious side as much as he can, nor does he mention their belief in a Messiah.

Messiah is Hebrew for 'the anointed one', in Greek *Christos*. Anointing with oil was an age-old Jewish practice to honour people; both kings and high priests were anointed in the ceremony of investment. The Jews held that one day such a Messiah would come, sent by God to be their king and deliverer, and to govern the whole earth. Ancient Jewish prophecies and all manner of portents seemed to suggest that 'The Last Times' or 'End of Days' had started, heralding the Messiah's coming and the establishment of God's kingdom. Hillel and his school might offer guidance for leading a quiet, honest, charitable life, to bring its rewards in Heaven, or perhaps on earth in the very long run. All that was humdrum stuff compared with the prophecies and expectations of God's instant deliverance from bondage.

For the Zealots these involved the violent destruction of Rome: the land must be purified at all costs from every taint of heathenism. Judas's battle-cry 'No Ruler but God' was echoed everywhere with fervent enthusiasm, especially by the poor of the cities and the small farmers. For the Zealots were in fact social revolutionaries, who also fought against greedy, corrupt, pro-Roman priests. Judas was in the direct tradition of his namesake, Judas Maccabaeus, Hammer of the Gentiles, who had united the nation, purified the Temple, defeated and defied an earlier heathen tyrant. Those who fought for God, the Temple and the Torah would surely receive miraculous aid from Heaven.

With Judas, however, these hopes were disappointed: the Romans caught him and put him to death. The morale of the religious nationalists sank sharply, and for the next decade Judaea was more or less peaceful. Storm-clouds gathered again during Tiberius's reign.

Tiberius has been unfairly blackened by two Roman historians, Tacitus and Suetonius (who wrote a little later than Josephus). In the main he carried on Augustus's policies skilfully and conscientiously, and did his best to promote honest, efficient government in the provinces. But in 26 he retired to Capri, and his favourites enjoyed too much power. A crop of conspiracies made him more gloomy and suspicious than before, increasing the tension at Rome.

Although he remained on friendly terms with several members of Herod's family, his policy towards the Jews was generally 'tough'. There were only two procurators of Judaea in the reign. Valerius Gratus affronted the people by changing the High Priest four times in three years, but then (in 18) put in Caiaphas, of New Testament fame or infamy. Valerius handed over in 26 to Pontius Pilate.

Friction between Pilate and the Jews was almost continuous. He often seemed to go out of his way to offend their scruples, and even when he built an aqueduct (part of which has survived) to give Jerusalem a good water supply, he used Temple funds. This caused riots and demonstrations, which he put down by force.

One of the rioters taken prisoner, according to Mark's Gospel, was Barabbas, presumably the man whose release the crowd are supposed to have demanded at the time of the Crucifixion. (It seems very unlikely, however, especially as Josephus does not mention it, that the procurator had such a custom of releasing a prisoner at the feast of Passover.)

Meanwhile, Philip and Antipas were keeping better order in their territories. Philip, a moderate and able ruler, who built a fine new city in the north, Caesarea Philippi, had no children. In 34, when he died, Tiberius annexed the region to Syria. Antipas, ruler of Galilee, also built cities, notably a new capital on the western shore of the Sea of Galilee, which he named Tiberias after the Emperor. John the Baptist denounced him for marrying Herodias, his dead brother's widow, and he kept John imprisoned in the fortress of Machaerus, but did not put him to death—until Herodias's daughter danced for her step-father and demanded John's head as her reward. Mark gives this incident but not her name; it is only from Josephus that we know she was called Salome.

To Herod Antipas, John was an agitator in the style of Judas of Galilee, whose religious fanaticism might spark off a new rebellion in his realm. Nor did John's death end the trouble, for many of his disciples were already supporting a young man from the Galilean town of Nazareth, who claimed to be the Messiah. Jesus began his ministry in dangerous territory, and we hear in Luke's Gospel how 'certain of the Pharisees' warned him to leave Galilee at once, 'for Herod will kill thee'. His defiant answer starts: 'Go ye, and tell that fox . . .'—but we are left wondering about the motives of these Pharisees friendly to Jesus who were trying to save his life.

The much-loved Hillel had died in 10 A.D., but his influence was still strong. Was it *his* followers who saw in this God-possessed young missionary a man after their own heart to bring the people back to true repentance; or was it the followers of the fierce Shammai who looked to Jesus as a new Zealot leader? The latter is more probable, for one of Jesus's own disciples was Simon the Zealot, and we are told in John's Gospel how on one occasion Jesus had to withdraw when a crowd was trying 'to make him king by force'. This followed the miraculous feeding of the five thousand assembled in the desert, perhaps with 'guerilla' intentions. Other Messianic claimants—Josephus refers to several—were also known as miracle-workers.

Professor Brandon, an eminent modern scholar, presents Jesus as sympathetic to the Zealots, and the social revolutionary from Nazareth certainly appealed to the poor and oppressed classes. When he came south to Jerusalem, he attacked the established order with a large following. In the scene where he overturned the tables of the moneychangers, he must have had moral, if not physical, support from the crowd in the Temple courts. On Brandon's interpretation of 'Render unto Caesar', he was with the Zealots again in ruling against the payment of tribute. Crucifixion was a specifically Roman form of execution, of which many Zealots were victims: the cross was a symbol of Zealot martyrdom before it became the sign of Christian salvation.

Even in the Gospel accounts, it often sounds as if Jesus's disciples took him for a Messiah who would introduce God's kingdom by the destruction of all enemies. Caiaphas was understandably afraid that this would bring down the wrath of Rome, so it was expedient that one man should die for the people rather than the whole nation perish. The initiative against Jesus seems to come wholly from the Sadducees and Temple officials; there is no hint in the Gospels, even if their authors suppressed the details, that Pilate was previously disturbed by this prophet's activities.

If only Josephus had reported in full the sequence of events leading up to the Crucifixion! But the Gospels are our only source, and they were all written at least a generation afterwards. Each of their authors was addressing different sets of people in different circumstances. Relying largely on oral traditions, they made unconscious anachronisms and also some deliberate changes in editing their stories. Mark, writing soon after the terrible 'Jewish War', did not want to remind anyone that Jesus was crucified as a Jewish rebel; so he did his best to make the main charge one of blasphemy rather than sedition, and to shift the responsibility from the Roman governor to the Jewish leaders. Matthew took the process a stage further, with fateful long-term results in the Christian attitude to the Jews down the centuries, by passing the blame to the whole Jewish people: 'His blood be on us, and on our children'.

In Brandon's view, then, the pacific Christ is an invention from later times. Clearly the Gospels have to some extent distorted the attitudes of the historic Jesus. All the same, the impression they leave of his personality, which cannot be completely unfounded, suggests a man who rejected the temptations of hatred, whether personal or national. This impression is heightened, of course, by the cry on the Cross, so unlike the Zealots in spirit: 'Father forgive them, for they know not what they do.'

As for Pilate, such a case involving the death penalty might well have put him in a dilemma. He had so often been in trouble with 'the natives' that when their leaders wanted him to try a fellow Jew it put him on the defensive: suppose he condemned an innocent man, it would be yet another count against him at Rome. His reluctance to pass the death sentence, therefore, sounds authentic, but his actions and motives during the trial remain obscure. Caiaphas was High Priest throughout Pilate's term of office, and so must have somehow got on with him, or he would have been deposed. Still, it is clear from Josephus as well as the Gospels that relations between procurator and Jewish leaders were always uneasy.

In 36, Pilate became involved with another prophet, but a Samaritan one, who promised to show his followers some sacred vessels buried by Moses on a holy mountain. The procurator set his soldiers on these Samaritans, killing many of them. Their leaders appealed to Vitellius, the governor of Syria, who at once dispatched an order deposing Pilate, sending him to Rome to stand trial. He was banished to a town in Gaul, and is generally supposed to have committed suicide there.

Vitellius himself came down to Judaea soon after this and tried to make a fresh start with the Jews. He abolished the

tax on the sale of agricultural produce at Jerusalem; he had
the High Priestly vestments transferred from the Antonia
fortress to the Temple; and, apparently on request from the
Sanhedrin, he deposed Caiaphas as High Priest, a concession
to nationalist sentiment.

Meanwhile Vitellius had become involved with Herod
Antipas. The ruler of Galilee—Josephus speaks of him as
just 'Herod'—was at war with an Arab king whose daughter
he had discarded in order to marry Herodias, and had been
badly defeated. 'Some of the Jews', Josephus reports in his
Antiquities, 'regarded the destruction of the army of Herod
as the work of God, who thus exacted very righteous retribution for John surnamed the Baptist. For Herod had slain
John—a good man who bade the Jews cultivate virtue by
justice towards each other and piety towards God and to
come to baptism; for immersion, he said, would only ap-
pear acceptable to God if practised ... for the purification
of the body, when the soul had already been thoroughly
cleansed by righteousness. Now when men flocked to him
... Herod feared that the powerful influence which he
exercised over men's minds might lead to some form of
revolt, for they seemed to do anything on his advice. To
forestall and kill him seemed far better than a belated
repentance when plunged in the turmoil of an insurrection.'

Did Josephus really write this passage? Probably he did.
For when he was writing, the Baptist's memory was no
longer a danger to Rome, and nothing extravagant is said
about him.

Antipas appealed for help to Tiberius, who instructed
Vitellius to send that insubordinate Arab king to Rome,
alive or dead. Marching down with two legions, Vitellius
was met by a deputation of Jews imploring him not to pass
through Judaea. He at once agreed, altering the army's

route so that it need not enter Judaea at all, and himself went to Jerusalem with Antipas, where he again behaved very graciously and received a warm welcome. He was still there when news came that Tiberius had died at Capri. Vitellius administered the oath of fidelity to the new Emperor, Gaius.

The accession of the son of the popular hero Germanicus brought high hopes to the Roman people. With a conciliatory governor of Syria, it looked as if even Judaea might be moving into a period of solid peace. This was in 37, the year when Josephus was born. But the early promise of the new reign soon lost its brightness in Rome, and even more for the Jews.

Coin of Herod Antipas

CHAPTER 4

JOSEPHUS AND THE JEWISH SECTS

The *Life* Josephus wrote is not an autobiography, unfortunately, since its purpose was to justify his conduct in the 'Jewish War', and nine tenths of it deal with that alone. With no outside references to his early years, and all we know about the boy Joseph Ben Matthias is what he says in the first paragraphs of the *Life*.

After talking proudly of his priestly ancestors and the royal blood on his mother's side, he goes on:—

'Distinguished as he was by his noble birth, my father Matthias was even more esteemed for his upright character, being among the most notable men in Jerusalem. Brought up with Matthias, my brother, I made great progress in my education, gaining a reputation for an excellent memory and understanding. While still a mere boy, about fourteen years old, I won universal applause for my love of letters; insomuch that the chief priests and the leading men of the city used constantly to come to me for precise information on some particular in our ordinances.'

What a prodigy! Josephus is not a trustworthy witness on himself, and at the end of his life it was unlikely that any of his readers would be able to contradict him. While the last sentence must therefore he taken with several

45

pinches of salt, we may credit him at least with being 'a very bright lad'.

There is a curious parallel with the one incident in the boyhood of Jesus of Nazareth which is recorded in the Gospels: the Passover pilgrimage to Jerusalem when the twelve-year-old Jesus was missed, to be discovered eventually by his anxious family in the Temple, 'sitting in the midst of the doctors, both hearing them and asking them questions'.

None of the Evangelists was trying to write a straight biography of Jesus, but there was evidently little tradition, oral or written, concerning Jesus as a boy; or they would surely have used it. Yet this story, which reveals so strikingly his sense of mission, is told only by Luke. Concerned to bridge the long gap between the birth and ministry of Jesus, Luke was conceivably influenced by memories of Josephus, from whom he seems to have gleaned material more than once.

The next paragraph in Josephus's *Life* is even more tantalising for its brevity. 'At about the age of sixteen I decided to gain personal experience of the several sects into which our nation is divided. These ... are three in number, the first that of the Pharisees, the second that of the Sadducees, and the third that of the Essenes. I thought that, after a thorough investigation, I should be in a position to choose the best. So I submitted myself to hard training and laborious exercises and passed through the three courses. Not content, however, with the experience thus gained, on hearing of one named Bannus, who lived in the wilderness, wearing only such clothing as trees provided, feeding on such things as grow of themselves, and using frequent ablutions of cold water, by day and night, for purity's sake, I became his devoted disciple. With him I lived for

46

three years and, having accomplished my purpose, returned to the city. Being now in my nineteenth year, I began to govern my life by the rules of the Pharisees.'

It was probably family tradition as much as his own convictions which made Joseph choose the Pharisees in the end. The long period spent with Bannus, a religious leader after the style of John the Baptist, comes as a surprise, for in later years Joseph showed no leanings towards austere holiness. It is a great pity that we do not have his reactions to a hermit's way of life or the stern rules of the Essenes. Perhaps not much of either rubbed off on him, although he retained an admiration for the Essenes, to judge by his long digression on the three sects in *The Jewish War*.

He starts with the Essenes, who 'profess a severer discipline' and 'are particularly attached to each other'. They avoid pleasure-seeking as a vice and regard temperance and mastery of the passions as virtue. Scorning wedlock, they pick out other men's children while still pliable and teachable, and fashion them after their own pattern ...

'Contemptuous of wealth, they believe in holding all goods in common ... Men to supervise the community's affairs are chosen for their tasks by a show of hands from the whole community.

'They possess no one city but everywhere have large colonies. When adherents arrive from elsewhere, all local resources are put at their disposal as if they were their own, and men they have never seen before entertain them like old friends. And so when they travel they carry no baggage at all, but only weapons to keep off bandits. In every town one of the order is appointed specially to look after strangers and issue clothing and provisions. In dress and personal appearance they are like children in the care of a stern tutor. Neither garments nor shoes are changed till they are dropping to pieces or worn out with age. Among themselves nothing is bought or sold; everyone gives what he has to anybody in need and receives from him in return something he himself can use. . . .

'Showing anger only when justified, they keep their tempers under control; they champion good faith and serve the cause of peace . . . They are wonderfully devoted to the work of ancient writers, choosing mostly books that can help soul and body; from them, in their anxiety to cure disease, they learn all about medicinal roots and the properties of stones.'

Admission to full membership of the sect took three years, and before it the initiate had to 'swear terrible oaths, first that he will revere the Godhead, secondly that he will deal justly with men, will injure no one either of his own accord or at another's bidding, will always hate the wicked and co-operate with the good, will keep faith at all times and with all men—especially with rulers, since all power is conferred by God. If he himself receives power, he will never abuse his authority, never by dress or extra ornament outshine those under him . . .

'They are long-lived, most of them passing the century, owing to the simplicity of their daily life, I suppose, and the regular routine. They despise danger and conquer pain by sheer will-power; death, if it comes with honour, they value more than life without end. Their spirit was tested to the utmost by the war with the Romans, who racked and twisted, burnt and broke them, subjecting them to every torture yet invented in order to make them blaspheme the Lawgiver or eat some forbidden food, but could not make them do either, or ever once fawn on their tormentors, or shed a tear. Smiling in their agony and gently mocking those who put them on the rack, they resigned their souls

48

in the joyous certainty that they would receive them back.

'It is indeed their unshakable conviction that bodies are corruptible ... whereas souls remain immortal ... once freed from the bonds of the flesh, as if released after years of slavery, they rejoice and soar aloft ...

'Some of them claim to foretell the future, after a lifelong study of sacred literature, purifications of different kinds and the wise sayings of prophets; rarely if ever do their predictions prove wrong.

'There is a second order of Essenes, which agrees with the other in its way of life, customs and rules, and differs only in its views on marriage. They think that the biggest thing in life—the continuance of the race—is forfeited by men who do not marry ...'

Josephus is clearly speaking from first-hand knowledge. Here again there may be a coincidence between his experience and that of Jesus, who quite possibly spent a period of his youth in such a community. Unlike the Essenes, of course, Jesus did not accept that loyalty to the Law meant withdrawal from common life; quite the reverse, as was sometimes held against him: '... a friend of publicans and sinners'. But the word Essene probably derives from the Aramaic *Chasya*, meaning 'saint', and by their saintly living, as in some of their teachings, they could have inspired the young man from Nazareth. They were healers—of bodies and souls—as he was to become. They had prophetic gifts. They also radiated an 'End of Days' or 'Last Times' atmosphere; this would encourage him to identify himself with the Messiah—who was to redeem a repentant Israel.

Josephus says there were about 4000 Essenes altogether. Ideas about the sect have changed as a result of the dramatic archaeological discoveries of the last twenty years.

In the early spring of 1947, a Bedouin boy was looking

for a lost goat in the bleak valley of Qumran on the north-western tip of the Dead Sea. A stone he threw into one of the caves hit something hollow, which frightened him so that he ran away. Later he climbed into the cave with a friend to explore, and they found clay jars with lids. Inside the jars were dark oblong lumps which they unrolled and saw were some sort of manuscripts. The boys could make nothing of them, but stuffed all they could into the loose folds of their robes, took them back to their tents, and in due course sold them to a merchant in Bethlehem. The manuscripts were the earliest find of what came to be known as the Dead Sea Scrolls, part of the large library of a monastic community, either Essene or closely related to the Essenes.

The cave and other nearby caves were searched, many more manuscripts came to light, but no one knew whether they were of any worth. The merchant sold the first scrolls in Jerusalem. When the manuscripts' value and importance were realised, he and other dealers made fortunes from them.

The first to be unrolled and examined in Jerusalem proved to be a scroll of the prophet Isaiah, dating from 100 B.C., a thousand years older than any previously known copy. Another was a document known as the New Covenant. The Hebrew word for covenant is equivalent to the Latin *testamentum*. Jeremiah had prophesied that God would make a New Covenant with His people, writing the Law not on stone (as at Sinai) but in their hearts. Jesus in the Last Supper spoke of 'my blood of the New Covenant, which is shed for many for the remission of sins'.

Passages in the scrolls seem like the Gospels. The famous 'I was hungry and you gave me food' is very closely paral-leled in a book used by the Qumran community. Jesus may have been quoting directly from this, adding his own moral, or else it was a memory of the Essenes introduced by Matthew. Yet, puzzlingly, the sect is nowhere mentioned in the New Testament, although Paul's Epistles also contain passages reminiscent of the Scrolls, and John the Baptist started baptising very near Qumran. Both he and Paul may well have had Essene connections.

Founded in the second century B.C., Qumran was devastated in 31 B.C. by an earthquake, and the community abandoned it. Reoccupied in 4 to 6 A.D., it remained in being till wiped out during the 'Jewish War'. No one tried to revive it or find its hidden sacred books.

Masada, the Zealots' first and last fortress during the war, became the scene of a massive 'dig' for eleven months between 1963 and 1965. Inspired by Yigael Yadin, the Israeli general and archaeologist, it was sponsored by his government, but had the voluntary labour of nearly 4000 men and women, Jews and Gentiles, from twenty-eight different countries. The expeditions achieved spectacular success, and among their finds was a scroll from Qumran.

One of the Scrolls found earlier pictured a mysterious Teacher of Righteousness persecuted and killed by his enemies, including a Wicked Priest—usually thought to be the Hasmonaean king Alexander Jannaeus. Nobody has convincingly identified the Teacher, who is very fierce and militant towards his enemies.

The Essenes had always been considered more or less pacifist, as we should guess from Josephus's remarks on their co-operation with rulers, 'since all power comes from God', and from Philo, who also wrote about the sect. Yet the Masada scroll suggests that survivors from Qumran joined Zealots in the fortress. The war against the Romans may, of course, have provided exceptional circumstances in which even Essenes felt they must fight.

The boy Joseph evidently went through his training in an environment markedly different from the one at Qumran. His and Philo's accounts, however, do remind one a little of the *kibbutzim* of modern Israel with their thorough-going communism—and of the early Christian communities.

After devoting so much space to the Essenes, Josephus gives a surprisingly brief and superficial summary of the other two sects:—

'... The Pharisees are held to be the most authoritative exponents of the Law and count as the leading sect. They put everything down to Fate or to God: the decision whether or not to do right rests mainly with men, but in every action Fate takes some part. Every soul is incorruptible, but only the souls of good men pass into other bodies, the souls of bad men being subjected to eternal punishment.

'The Sadducees ... deny Fate altogether, and hold that God is incapable of either committing sin or seeing it; they say that men are free to choose between good and evil, and each individual must decide which he will follow. The permanence of the soul, punishments in Hades, and rewards they deny utterly.

'Again, Pharisees are friendly to one another and try to live harmoniously with the general public, but Sadducees, even towards each other, show a more disagreeable spirit, and in their relations with men like themselves they are as harsh as they might be to foreigners.'

If our knowledge of the Sadducees were confined to this passage, it would be hard to understand how and why they still held their position of an aristocratic 'establishment'. Although often arrogant and reactionary, they had a function of tremendous importance, because they officiated in the Temple services, ritual and law courts. They could claim to be responsible for maintaining public order and assuring the continuity of national life, especially the Temple's survival as the world centre of the Jewish faith. If the Romans allowed independence to the Jewish courts and also freedom of worship, the Sadducees would co-operate with Roman power in secular affairs.

For the Pharisees there were no 'secular affairs'; God's Law covered the whole of life, offering instruction and guidance in every situation. Hillel and many Pharisees knew that some commandments were far more important than others, but to try to keep them all was meant to be a joy, not a burden—part of the privilege in having a unique and lasting connection with God. Local synagogue officials and teachers, if not members of the sect themselves, were much influenced by the Pharisees' beliefs and practice.

We are so used to the denunciations in the Gospels that it is hard to see the Pharisees as protectors of Jewish ethical and social values. With the emphasis on strict observances and ritual purity, there was a danger, obviously, of hypocrisy and self-righteousness, of obeying the letter of the law rather than its spirit. The best Pharisees were well aware of this danger and guarded against it; many others succumbed. But we should remember that the Evangelists, writing after the war, were concerned to blacken the Pharisees, so as to dissociate themselves from the Jews as a whole.

Jesus probably respected many Pharisees. He was brought up at least partly in their tradition, and stressed that he came to bring the Law to its full meaning, not to destroy it. But it seems likely that the Pharisees on the whole were not expecting a personal Messiah in the near future. From the writings of Josephus we should get little idea that many people in Judaea had such strong hopes of seeing God's kingdom established. These hopes were much weakened by the way the 'Jewish War' ended, with no supernatural deliverance in sight. Perhaps Josephus never took them very seriously, but it is strange, all the same, that he never refers to the new Jewish sect which grew so fast during his boyhood—the Nazarenes, as the first Christians were called.

What happened during those fateful days of the Jewish Passover near the end of Tiberius's reign (the exact year is uncertain)? Even if the Resurrection story was due to collective hallucinations or unexplained psychic phenomena, or the whole thing was an invention, something extraordinary must have occurred: the first outcrop of the Christian faith is on any count a mystery.

Crucifixion was not only an agonising death but also utter degradation in Jewish eyes. A crucified Messiah was a contradiction in terms, or had been till then. Yet the small band of dispirited leaderless men and women, with all their hopes shattered, were suddenly transformed by the dynamic conviction that their leader had conquered death and would soon be returning in glory to establish God's kingdom and execute judgment. They saw portents, grew ecstatic and 'spoke with tongues'. They carried on the healing ministry started by Jesus, preached the risen Messiah, and very quickly gained a large following, which became known as an assembly—Greek *ekklesia*—later called church. (from a Greek word meaning the Lord's house).

It was not a new religion, but the Jewish faith made concrete. The Nazarenes claimed to be the Jews of true loyalty who had acknowledged the Lord's anointed when he first came. At his second coming he would punish those who had delivered him over to the Roman governor and were responsible for his death. That meant especially the Sadducees and high Temple officials, and the Jewish masses were very ready to go along with an attack on *them*.

The Sadducees counter-attacked hard, but at first the Pharisee Gamaliel, Hillel's grandson, successfully defended the Nazarenes in council with words that ring down the centuries: 'Keep away from these men and let them alone: for if this plan or this undertaking is of men, it will fail; but if it is of God, you will not be able to overthrow them. You might even be found opposing God.'

A little later, however, one of the seven 'deacons' the Nazarenes had chosen was stoned to death after a trial by the Sanhedrin: the charge against Stephen, first Christian martyr, was preaching against the Temple and the Law. After this, a persecution of the infant church at Jerusalem took place. The faithful were scattered to other parts of Judaea and beyond, which helped to spread the Gospel ('Good News') they carried with them. Philip, another of the deacons, converted many of the Samaritans, and for the Nazarenes the old breach between Jew and Samaritan was healed for good. Later, Philip converted a high official of the Queen of Ethiopia, thus taking the Gospel to 'the uttermost part of the earth'.

According to *The Acts*, the Apostles stayed in Jerusalem. Among them Peter and the brothers James and John were pre-eminent. The other acknowledged leader was James, brother of Jesus, unmentioned in the Gospels, nor does his primacy receive any explanation in *The Acts*. But Jewish history has many examples of such 'dynastic succession': if Jesus was the true king, after his death his brother would automatically take over authority.

Stephen had probably offended many of his fellow Jews by what they thought excessive readiness to share the Gospel with Gentiles. One of those who had persecuted him and the Church was Saul, a devout Pharisee from Tarsus in Cilicia (now southern Turkey), where Antony had his memorable first meeting with Cleopatra—when she sailed up the Cydnus in her 'barge of burnished gold'. Antony had made Tarsus a free self-governing city.

Saul inherited Roman citizenship, and was known to non-Jews as Paul (Paulus), although as a strict Jew he preferred to use his Jewish name. He was highly educated, and we learn in *The Acts* that he studied under Gamaliel. He was a man of strong emotions and enthusiasms, a visionary, and possibly an epileptic. Moved by Stephen's dying words of forgiveness, and by an instinctive sympathy—till then unrecognised—for those he was attacking, Saul had his dramatic experience on the Damascus road, which led to a complete change of heart and mind.

He soon became a leading Nazarene, and from now on kept to the name Paul. The Pharisees had always been eager to expand indefinitely the number of 'God-fearers', and Paul, a Pharisee steeped in Jewish culture, naturally conceived his mission to be that of an apostle to the Gentiles. But this sharpened a division of opinion in the Jerusalem Church on the correct attitude towards Gentile converts. It was a point on which the Messiah's teaching could be interpreted in different ways.

We cannot expect all the sayings of Jesus recorded in the Gospels to be accurate and authentic. The most we can hope for is an impression of the general line taken by a unique character on the questions which specially concerned him. By this reckoning Jesus was a good Jew who shared with many other Rabbis an emphasis on observing the spirit rather than the letter of the Law. Socially and ethically in the Jewish prophetic tradition, he was against the wealthy, self-righteous and conventional, and against a corrupt 'establishment'; he felt warmly towards the common people, social outcasts, and sinners who repented. But he believed he was the Jewish Messiah, speaking primarily to Jews. Among them he looked for enough apprentices to a new way of life for Israel to be transformed. A transformed Israel would transform the world—if there was time for that before the End of Days.

Still, Jesus had not confined the use of his remarkable healing powers to helping Jews, and his whole personality radiated a love for humanity regardless of race. This went with insistence that loving your neighbour was more important than ritual, and the promise that 'my burden is easy'—in contrast to the rigorous demands faced by a convert in fully observing the Jewish law. These things made a strong appeal to the Gentiles. Their readiness to respond, combined with the Gospel's rejection by many Jews, encouraged Paul to adapt its content, for the most part unconsciously. The process had started whereby a Jewish Messiah turned into a spiritual saviour of all mankind.

But it was the nationalist side of the new faith that most alarmed the authorities, both Roman and Jewish. One inscription shows that the death penalty was decreed for violation of tombs, perhaps an attempt to stop further resurrection stories. Certainly the idea of an insubstantial leader risen from the dead, who therefore could not be touched, was new and disconcerting. The leaders who were not ghosts could be more easily dealt with, and in 44, as *The Acts* records, King Agrippa, Herod's grandson, 'put forth his hands to afflict certain of the church. And he killed James the brother of John with the sword. And when he saw that it pleased the Jews, he proceeded to seize Peter also.'

If John died at the same time as James, as some scholars believe, it is strange that this is not recorded in *The Acts*, which contains no further mention of him. Peter, too, after the story of his miraculous escape from prison, disappears from the picture: 'He departed and went to another place.' This was probably Alexandria, a city Paul never visited; Peter may not have wanted another leading apostle, with whom he sometimes disagreed, to encroach on his territory. Meanwhile James, brother of Jesus, was left as acknowledged head of the Church.

The expression 'it pleased the Jews' may well be a deliberate exaggeration; it was mainly the Sadducees who would be pleased by an attack on the Jerusalem Church. There is no evidence of any further specific attack on it for twenty years, and after this crisis it probably lost some of its revolutionary character. Other Pharisees besides Paul came into it, and it was generally sympathetic to the lower order of priests. These tended, admittedly, to be radical in politics, partly because the priestly aristocracy often cut off their income from tithes (special dues payable to all priests), leaving them in poverty. That was another bone of contention between Sadducees and Pharisees, with the Nazarenes supporting the latter. When he finally joined the Pharisees at the age of nineteen, the young Joseph Ben Matthias must have often come into contact with the Nazarenes.

In his youth, however, the split between the two schools of the Pharisees was growing steadily wider. By temperament he was more attracted to Hillel's school than to Shammai's. You led your life according to the Law, quietly extending Jewish influence by the example set, trying even under foreign rule to improve conditions for the people. From his later life we might guess that he was more concerned with ritual and observance than with social justice, readier to conform than to protest. Yet the next information on himself in the *Life* shows him in a very positive light, and suggests that he had both a high reputation and plenty of courage:—

'Soon after I had completed my twenty sixth year, it fell to my lot to go up to Rome . . . At the time when Felix was procurator of Judaea, some priests I knew, very excellent men, were on a slight and trifling charge sent by him in bonds to Rome to render an account to Caesar (Nero). I was anxious to find some means of delivering them, more especially as I learnt that, even in affliction, they had not forgotten the pious practices of religion, and supported themselves on figs and nuts . . .' (other food would have been impure).

For the moment we will leave Joseph setting out on his errand of mercy, to see how the Jewish people were faring while he grew up. Their 'cold war' with Rome continued— except during the brief reign of Agrippa, last king of the Jews.

Coin of King Agrippa I

CHAPTER 5

LAST KING
OF THE JEWS

Grandson of Herod the Great, Agrippa was brought up at the Roman court with Drusus, Tiberius's son. Clever and charming, he entertained lavishly, and in his early thirties had run through a fortune—when his friend Drusus died prematurely and he lost the Emperor's favour. After a chequered career in Palestine and Syria, Agrippa managed to regain that favour for a while, securing the friendship of Gaius, now the heir apparent. Then he blundered once more. After giving Gaius a very good dinner one night, he finished (Josephus tells us) 'by stretching out his hands and openly praying that Tiberius might die soon so that he could see Gaius lord of the world. One of the servants passed this on to Tiberius, who was furious and had Agrippa locked up.' He remained under strict confinement for six months until Tiberius died.

Gaius at once released Agrippa and made him king of Philip's territory; Philip had died just before this. Then Herod Antipas came to Rome asking to be made king too. But Agrippa, with whom he had quarrelled, brought charges against him which Gaius accepted. Antipas was banished to Spain, and Agrippa was given his realm as well. Agrippa's

Medallion of Herod the Great.

Herod Antipas and Herodias from a thirteenth-century mosaic in the Baptistry at Florence.

Christ before Caiaphas. A painting by Fra Angelico in the Accademia in Florence.

St Paul. A mural in the Hypogeum vaults near the Ponte Maggiore in Rome. This is believed

influence with the new Emperor was to prove very valuable for the Jews.

Like his predecessor, Gaius has suffered at the hands of Roman historians, and is best known as an emperor with delusions of grandeur, so mad that he made his horse a consul; perhaps he merely commented that he would as soon appoint his horse a consul as a particular Senator. Yet according to Josephus he ruled well for two years, and in the first few months he was universally popular. Even after this 'honeymoon period', when he did everything to humiliate the Senate, his government of the Empire remained able enough, except for a clash with the Jews over his own 'divinity'.

In the east, Roman generals were often identified with gods. Antony, one of Gaius's great-grandfathers, had appeared at Athens in the costume of Dionysus. Augustus had many altars and temples dedicated to him, and encouraged worship of the imperial house with the goddess Roma. From this it was only a small step for emperors to become gods during their lifetime, which caused no offence in most of the Empire; and once Gaius had laid claim to divinity, leading men had to take the claim very seriously.

But the Supreme Being of the Jews was a jealous God. *They* could not accept any of the local deities, let alone Caesar-worship. They offered sacrifices twice a day for the Emperor's welfare, and until now that was considered a sufficient sign of their loyalty. Gaius, however, rashly tried to force the issue.

The trouble began in Alexandria, sparked off by the arrival of Agrippa on the way to his kingdom. The Jews received him in triumph, their enemies demonstrated against him. Riots followed, and turned into a violent attack on the Jews, openly encouraged by the Prefect of Egypt. Thousands

61

were killed, synagogues desecrated, and statues of the Emperor placed in them. Agrippa sent bitter complaints to Gaius, who banished the Prefect. But Gaius did not reach a decision between two rival deputations from Alexandria, and it was left to Claudius to make an official settlement of their differences. The Jewish deputation was led by Philo, the Gentile one by a writer called Apion. Half a century later, in his defence of the Jews against abuse by the Greeks, Josephus used Apion's name as prototype of Greek 'anti-Semites'.

What had been done at Alexandria encouraged the Gentile inhabitants of Jamnia, a town on the coast of Palestine, to put up an altar to Gaius in a synagogue. The Jews at once destroyed it. To punish all Jews for this insult, the Emperor sent orders to Petronius, governor of Syria, that a colossal gilt statue of himself as Jupiter should be erected in the Temple at Jerusalem.

Petronius did his best to 'stall', knowing that the Jews would never tolerate such sacrilege, and (according to Philo) warned Gaius that they would revolt. Tacitus says they did take up arms, but Josephus gives their reaction in terms of non-violent resistance. Many thousands came to Petronius begging him not to put up the statue, but he said he must obey his orders—using almost the same words (in Josephus's account) as the centurion in the Gospels: . . .'for I am under authority as well as you'. They insisted that he would first have to 'sacrifice the entire Jewish nation'; and that they presented themselves, their wives and their children, 'ready for the slaughter'. Eventually Petronius took an extremely brave decision—to tell the Emperor that his orders could not be carried out.

Meanwhile Agrippa had been active in Rome. He first wrote to Gaius, then gave a sumptuous banquet for him. In high good humour, the Emperor told Agrippa to ask for anything he wanted. Agrippa repeated the request in his letter that the order for the statue should be cancelled; the request was granted. Jews everywhere remembered his courage gratefully: such personal intervention with the temperamental Emperor was obviously a very risky business.

On receiving the dispatch from Syria, in fact, Gaius was furious and sent Petronius orders to kill himself. Luckily for the latter, 'the bearers of this message were weather-bound for three months at sea, while others, who brought the news of the death of Gaius, had a fortunate passage'. They arrived a month sooner, and Petronius was saved. So were the Jews, who of course saw the death of Gaius—in 41 A.D.—as God's vengeance.

He had been assassinated. The Senators had long resented their lack of political power. Now they rejoiced at the tyrant's fall, and hoped the Republic would be restored. They were foiled by the personal body-guard of the Emperors, the Praetorian Guard, who dragged out of hiding their own nominee and forced the Senators at sword point to agree to his becoming the new Emperor. This was Claudius, Gaius's uncle, and a boyhood friend of Agrippa's. Both Claudius and the Senate consulted Agrippa, and he acted very skilfully as go-between, enabling Claudius to accede without bloodshed.

Claudius had been an awkward, unprepossessing young man, who was thought slightly feeble-minded and had scarcely any experience of public life. On the whole, however, he proved a careful and competent administrator, although he let himself be dominated by an inner cabinet of freedmen and by each of his two wives in turn. One was Messalina—eventually put to death for conspiracy, the other was Agrippina, mother of Nero. The in-fighting between wives and freedmen led to many crimes, but these disturbed mainly Rome and life at the court. Still, the freedmen's influence added to corruption and misgovernment in the provinces. They were offered and took lavish bribes, becoming multi-millionaires. They were also anti-Jewish, which later in Claudius's reign helped to bedevil relations between Rome and the Jews even more.

At first, however, there was a harmony in those relations never to be repeated. Claudius rewarded Agrippa for his help in the accession by making him king of a greater Judaea, including all his grandfather's territory. Agrippa, called in inscriptions 'Friend of Rome and Friend of Caesar', was more successful than Herod in keeping the support of most of the Jews as well. Though generous to pagan cities such as Berytus (Beirut), in Judaea at least he was a pious Jew, paid respect to the Pharisees, made Jerusalem his chief residence, and sacrificed regularly in the Temple.

He even showed signs of nationalist independence, and began, for instance, to reconstruct Jerusalem's north wall. Had the wall been completed—Josephus comments—it would have been impregnable; but when the foundations had been laid, Agrippa thought better of it and stopped building, perhaps after a friendly warning from Claudius.

The King's influence was evident in Claudius's settlement of the conflict at Alexandria. A copy of the Emperor's letter to its citizens still exists. He told the Gentiles not to interfere with the Jews' privileges, recognised by long tradition, which he now fully confirmed. But he also warned the Jews against trying to obtain more privileges, and against increasing their numbers by taking in Jews from other parts of Egypt or from Syria—lest he should be compelled to punish them for 'encouraging a general plague throughout the world'.

In Judaea—free from tribute, Roman legions and tax-collectors—moderate opinion was well satisfied. Fanatics who could not accept a Jewish king's rule were likely to leave the country and pursue abroad the missionary activities which the Roman government found so dangerously subversive. Among such fanatics were the Nazarenes, or Christians, as they now came to be called in the Greek-speaking Empire. The 'Jews from Syria' might well refer to this new sect, which was spreading fast in Antioch, the Empire's third city; especially as Agrippa had adopted such a tough policy towards it.

In *The Acts* account, Agrippa was soon punished for laying hands on the apostles. In the spring of 44, he went to Caesarea to preside at thanksgiving celebrations for Claudius's return to Rome after a successful campaign in Britain. The inhabitants gave Agrippa a rapturous reception and hailed him as a god; the scene is recorded by Josephus as well as in *The Acts*. He failed to rebuke them, accepted their homage, and almost at once developed a mysterious illness, possibly due to poisoning. He died five days later, at the age of fifty-four.

All the old conflicts between Jews and Gentiles immediately broke out again. The Greeks in Caesarea and Sebaste, who had joined in the flattery, now insulted Agrippa's memory; worse still, Claudius's freedmen persuaded the Emperor that the government of Judaea could not be given to Agrippa's son, also called Agrippa, a boy of seventeen. So the country returned to direct Roman rule.

The sun which had briefly shone for the Jewish people with much of its former splendour, now began to go down fast. King Agrippa had allowed them to enjoy the trade, security and all the benefits of the Roman Peace without any of its provocations and humiliations. It was the last time an independent Jewish state existed in Palestine until just over 1900 years later.

CHAPTER 6

PROCURATORS
AND GUERILLAS

The return of the procurators meant a revival of many Jewish grievances, with the result that Zealots regained support and incentive for rebellion. Fadus, the first procurator, dealt with them ruthlessly; and as a sign that the Romans were once again masters, he demanded custody of the High Priestly vestments. The governor of Syria brought a large force down to overawe opposition, but the Jewish leaders were allowed to send a deputation to the Emperor, which had support from the young Agrippa. He was living at Rome, and already showed some of his father's skill in diplomacy.

Claudius handed the ambassadors a copy of an edict addressed to 'the magistrates, senate, people, and whole nation of the Jews'—an extremely gratifying and conciliatory form of address—cancelling Fadus's order, and telling them they had Agrippa to thank for this. Compliments were also paid to his uncle, yet another Herod, then King of Chalcis in Syria. Herod was now given custody of the vestments and made treasurer of the Temple, with the appointment of the High Priests in his hands.

In 48, when Herod died, these powers were given to Agrippa, who was also made king of Chalcis. Three years later Claudius transferred him to Philip's former territory, and he afterwards received a strip of Galilee and part of Peraea. So King Agrippa II ruled over a large though scattered territory on the outer corners of Judaea. Except in Galilee, almost all the kingdom's inhabitants were pagan, and he was generous to pagan cities. Like his father, however, he also did his best for the Jews of the Dispersion; while his Temple duties, with a residence in a palace right by the Temple, made him an important supporter of Rome in Jerusalem itself.

For the next procurator Claudius chose a lapsed Jew called Tiberius Alexander, a nephew of Philo, who was also Agrippa's brother-in-law. He later became Prefect of Egypt and kept his position under Vespasian, so Josephus had to be careful what he said, and merely records that 'Tiberius Alexander, by abstaining from all interference with the customs of the country, kept the nation at peace.' He continued the policy of suppressing the Zealots, and had two sons of Judas of Galilee crucified. The peace broke down under Cumanus, who succeeded Tiberius.

Trouble started at the Jewish Passover of 48 A.D. with an insulting gesture from one of the guard on the roof of the Temple's portico. The crowd demanded of Cumanus that the soldier be punished, and some hotheads began stoning the guard. Cumanus sent for reinforcements. In Josephus's account, 'when these troops were pouring into the porticoes, the Jews were seized with panic and turned to fly from the Temple and make their way into the town. But such violence was used as they pressed round the exits that they were trodden under foot and crushed to death by one another; over thirty thousand perished, and the feast was turned into mourning for the whole nation and for every household into lamentation.'

The number of the dead is incredible; Josephus's figures are often wildly exaggerated. But he describes the scene so vividly—in his poetic, almost biblical style—that it suggests he may for the first time be writing as an eye-witness, its horror branded on the eleven-year-old boy's memory.

Then 'brigands', probably Zealots, robbed one of the Emperor's slaves on a main highway. Cumanus had the neighbouring villages sacked and their notables arrested for protecting the culprits. In one village a soldier found 'a copy of the sacred law, tore the book in pieces and flung it into the fire. At that the Jews were roused as though . . . their whole country . . . had been consumed in the flames.' There was a mass complaint to Cumanus at Caesarea, and the procurator yielded to a demand for the punishment of the offender, who was 'led to execution through the ranks of his accusers. On this the Jews withdrew'.

Then some Samaritans attacked a band of Galilean Jews going to Jerusalem for a festival. This time Cumanus ignored Jewish protests, and after savage reprisals by the Zealots he set out with a troop of cavalry to help the Samaritans, killing and taking prisoner many Zealots. As for the rest of the Jews, 'who had rushed to war with the Samaritans, the magistrates of Jerusalem rushed after them, clad in sackcloth and with ashes on their heads, and implored them to return home and not . . . to bring down the wrath of the Romans on Jerusalem'. So the angry crowds dispersed, but guerilla activity became more intensive all over the country.

Both Jews and Samaritans appealed to the governor of Syria, who sent notables from each side to Rome along with Cumanus and Celer, the procurator's aide. Claudius heard the two delegations and Cumanus in the presence of Agrippa, 'who made a spirited defence on behalf of the Jews'. The

Emperor 'condemned the Samaritans, ordered three of their most prominent men to be executed, and banished Cumanus'. Celer was sent back in chains to Jerusalem, to be dragged round the streets and then beheaded.

That Agrippa had again won the day for the Jews was partly due to the support of Agrippina, Claudius's second wife, now very powerful at court, especially as she was having an affair with Pallas, one of Claudius's 'inner cabinet' freedmen. The Jews had high hopes, therefore, of Felix, brother of Pallas, who was sent out as the new Procurator. They were soon disillusioned: in office for eight years (from 52 to 60), he proved as brutal and corrupt as any, exercising a king's authority, says Tacitus, with a slave's mentality. He married Agrippa's sister Drusilla, however, which at least gave him some contact with Jewish interests.

Meanwhile Claudius died (in 54) after a reign of thirteen years. He may have been poisoned by Agrippina, who had ensured the succession for her son Nero. Nero has gone down to history as a monster of cruelty because of his crimes against his family and his persecution of the Christians. But the first five years of his reign were afterwards considered a period of extremely good government. The credit for this is usually given to his chief advisers, the Stoic philosopher Seneca and Burrus, the prefect of the Praetorian Guard. Like Claudius, Nero gave large sums of money to these troops, recognising how much his safety depended on them. Their prefect was always one of the key figures in the state.

Seneca was bitterly anti-Jewish, declaring that 'the customs of that most criminal nation have gained such strength that they have now been received in all nations. The conquered have given laws to the conquerors.' So although Nero continued to show favour to Agrippa, imperial policy towards the Jews became more hostile again. Felix in Judaea made new efforts to stamp out the Zealots, who clearly enjoyed wide popular support—as Josephus cannot help admitting: 'Felix took prisoner Eleazar, the brigand chief ... with many of his associates, and sent them for trial to Rome. Of the brigands whom he crucified, and of the common people convicted of complicity with them ... the number was incalculable.'

'But while the country was thus cleared of these pests,' Josephus goes on, 'a new species of bandits was springing up in Jerusalem, the so-called *sicarii*, who committed murders in broad daylight in the heart of the city.' The word came from *sica* (sickle), and he explains that 'the festivals were their special seasons, when they would mingle with the crowd, carrying short daggers under their clothes, with which they stabbed their enemies. Then ... they joined in the cries of indignation and so were never discovered. The first they assassinated was Jonathan the high priest; after his death there were many daily murders. The panic created was more alarming than the calamity itself ... Men kept watch at a distance on their enemies and would not trust even their friends when they approached.'

Jonathan was stabbed in the Temple itself, and Josephus insists repeatedly that the Zealots were largely responsible, through their crimes and sacrilege, for the Temple's destruction. He then describes 'another body of villains, with purer hands but more impious intentions, who no less than the assassins ruined the peace of the city. Deceivers and impostors, under the pretence of divine inspiration fostering revolutionary changes, they persuaded the multitude to act like madmen, and led them out into the desert under the belief that God would give them tokens of deliverance.'

This has sometimes been taken as referring to the Nazarenes, but it seems unlikely. They were probably new Messianic claimants and miracle-workers, the 'false prophets' mentioned in Matthew's Gospel who 'would show great signs . . . they shall say unto you, Behold he is in the wilderness'.

Josephus uses the same phrase, 'false prophet', of an Egyptian Jew who 'collected a following of about 30,000 dupes' (*The Acts* gives the number as 4000) and led them from the desert to the Mount of Olives, intending to storm Jerusalem. Anticipating the attack, Felix 'went to meet him with the Roman heavy infantry, the whole population joining him in the defence . . . The Egyptian escaped with a few of his followers; most of his force were killed or taken prisoners; the rest dispersed and stealthily escaped to their several homes.' Paul, asked after his arrest whether he was this Egyptian, gave his proud reply: 'I am a Jew, of Tarsus in Cilicia, a citizen of no mean city . . .'

The impostors and brigands banded together, says Josephus, urging large numbers to revolt and assert their independence, and threatening to kill any who submitted to Roman domination. 'Distributing themselves in companies throughout the country, they looted the houses of the wealthy, murdered their owners, and set the villages on fire . . .'

When at the age of nineteen, after his period in the wilderness with Bannus the hermit, Josephus returned to Jerusalem and joined the Pharisees, this was the atmosphere prevailing. Probably he soon became prominent in the pro-Roman 'peace party'. Writing after the 'Jewish War', he tried to show most of the Jews in Judaea were loyal to Rome (the whole population joined Felix in defending Jerusalem), but were terrorised by the brigands. There are many painful modern parallels of 'collaborators' rewriting history

72

for their conquerors. Josephus was more honest than most in the extent to which he admitted the mass support achieved by the Resistance Movement.

Bitterly divided in most of Judaea, the Jews were united at Caesarea, where they demanded a greater share than the Greeks in running the city. They were richer and more numerous, but the Greeks had the support of the soldiers, mainly recruited from Syria. Riots and street battles became almost continuous, and eventually Felix sent deputations from both sides to Nero. The Jewish deputation impeached him, however, and he was recalled to Rome. Porcius Festus, who replaced him, was evidently more moderate and honest than most procurators, and had some success in keeping down the Zealots.

There was a lull at Caesarea while Nero heard the two sides. But the Syrian delegation bribed his Secretary for Greek affairs, and Pallas, Felix's brother, was serving on the court. The Emperor gave his verdict in favour of the Gentiles, depriving the Jewish inhabitants of Caesarea of their equal status. A severe blow to Jewish pride and interests, it roused the Zealots to new fury and undid much of Festus's work.

Agrippa had lost his influence at Rome through the death of Agrippina, the Emperor's mother, in 59. Nero had her murdered, with the encouragement of his mistress Poppaea, whom he later married—Otho, Poppaea's husband, was sent away to govern an African province. Although Poppaea was involved in the murder, Josephus describes her as a 'religious woman', which suggests she was sympathetic towards Judaism, a remarkable sign of Jewish missionary success in high places. But she could not be expected to favour Agrippina's protégé, so Agrippa was at pains to greet Festus, the new Procurator, as soon as possible, and establish friendly relations with him. Paying his respects, the King was accompanied by his sister Berenice, who lived at his court —some said incestuously with her brother.

Antiquities records a dispute in which Agrippa and the Procurator were ranged against the High Priests, and their friendship is also attested in *The Acts* during the long-drawn-out trial of Paul. But for the latter we must go back to developments in the young Christian Church since Peter's flight from Jerusalem.

Coin of King Agrippa II

CHAPTER 7

NEED CHRISTIANS
BE JEWS?

For the first decades of the Church's history our two main sources are Paul's Epistles and *The Acts of the Apostles*. The Epistles are the earliest New Testament writings, but some have been preserved in a very unsatisfactory state, and Luke probably did not know of them when he wrote *The Acts* some forty years later. The two accounts show marked discrepancies, and what happened may have been something like this.

Paul's reputation was for quite a while under an eclipse. After the decline of the Jerusalem Church, Luke composed *The Acts* to publicise Paul as the great Apostle, giving an idealised picture of Christianity's God-directed progress from its origins in provincial Jerusalem to its solid establishment in Rome, the capital of the Gentile world—with harmony inside the Church as well. The Epistles, on the other hand, leave the impression of an atmosphere full of bitter conflict, centring on Paul's authority and the conditions for admitting Gentiles into the Christian community.

The Epistles show little concern with anything Jesus said or did while alive; all the stress is on the crucifixion and resurrection. Paul's position was based on personal experience of the risen Christ, who had given him his mission to the Gentiles. When the 'second coming' was delayed, perhaps to allow the Gentiles time to catch up in faith and penitence, it separated the Messiah still further from the Jesus of Nazareth who was to restore the kingdom of Israel on earth. But this more mystical belief in the Saviour of all mankind was just as dynamic. Paul and many of his converts had a tremendous sense of God's power flowing into their lives. In the Judaism of the time, the Messiah meant something only for the nation as a whole and also for world history (the 'Messianic Age'). The Messiah of Paul's vision was more concerned with saving *individuals*: the term *Christ* (Greek for *Messiah*) became a mere title.

The next stage in the Apostle's thought was a conviction that Jesus was more than Man, was God made flesh, and 'the Son of God'—an idea completely foreign to the Jews, for whom an unbridgable gulf existed between God and Man. But sons of gods, gods dying and reborn, often associated with fertility rites, were quite familiar to the Gentiles, through the myths of Greece and Rome and the many mystery religions which offered salvation to the unhappy and oppressed.

Although Paul talked much of the Holy Spirit as well, he had no full-blown doctrine of a Trinity; God for him was still the One God peculiar to the Jews. His teaching contained other specifically Jewish features: avoidance of idolatry, strong social and ethical demands, a sense that historical events showed the divine will, and a readiness to see consolation coming out of disaster (the crucifixion). As a Pharisee he believed in resurrection as well, but shifted the hopes based on it to the Greek environment in which he spent most of his days. Through Christ's crucifixion and resurrection everyone who believed could be saved, born again, and triumph over death.

76

The first Christian communities consisted largely of artisans, freedmen and slaves, attracted by teachings of social equality, and of women—no circumcision problem for *them*. God-fearers also liked the promise of salvation on an equality with full Jews. Again, it was a great relief if Christians could enjoy what was called 'table fellowship', whereas Jews were prevented by their dietary laws from having meals with Gentiles. As for the Gentile converts, they were delighted to be told by Paul that God would not judge them on how far they kept all the complicated rules of daily life: 'If justification were through the Jewish law, then Christ died to no purpose.'

Expectation of the second coming made some of them careless of present duties, and Paul realised they were giving the faith a bad name. This can be seen from reproaches in the Epistles against 'drop-outs' ('He who will not work, neither shall he eat') and warnings to those who indulge in a long list of vices that they will not inherit the kingdom of God. If his converts let him down by misconduct and immorality, it was a serious weakness for him when dealing with the strong opposition among his fellow Christians.

To the Nazarenes it was almost blasphemous to assert that the crucifixion of Israel's Messiah was a divine act to save Gentiles. The Jerusalem Church was still the acknowledged authority, its members stayed loyal to the Temple, the dietary laws and circumcision. They believed the Messiah had come, and would soon return. Till then they could only wait in hope, keeping the Law which he had said he would bring to its full meaning. After large-scale conversion of Gentiles had become an accomplished fact, they did their best to control it and keep it within bounds.

The Acts' account presents differences of opinion as settled at a special council of Church leaders in Jerusalem (in 49), with all the concessions made to Paul. But James and Peter probably made far more reservations than we hear about. Many of Paul's quarrels with the Jews during his missionary journeys concerned Gentile converts, for whom he implicitly claimed the privileges granted by Rome to the Jews. Meanwhile Roman officials in the Empire still suspected the Christians as men 'that had turned the world upside down', acting 'contrary to the decrees of Caesar, saying that there is another king, one Jesus'.

There had been a Christian community at Rome itself before Paul went there, and it may have become divided between Paul's teachings and those of the Jerusalem church. In 49, Claudius temporarily closed certain synagogues and banished foreign Jews from the capital. We hear of it both in *The Acts* and from Suetonius, who says that the Jews were 'continually raising tumults at the instigation of Chrestus' (almost certainly a misspelling of 'Christ'). This is one of the two earliest references in pagan sources to Christians in Rome. If only it had been more detailed! Were the tumults caused by tensions between different Christian factions, between Christians and Jews, or by Christian incitements to rebellion? No one can say.

The other early reference is in the *Annals* of Tacitus, who was strongly prejudiced against the Christians. By the execution of Christ, 'the sect of which he was a founder received a blow which for a time checked the growth of a dangerous superstition; but it broke out again, and spread with increased vigour, not only in Judaea, the soil that gave it birth, but even in the city of Rome, the common sewer into which everything infamous and abominable flows like a torrent from all quarters of the world'.

Tacitus was writing fifty years later, but even in Claudius's time Christianity was recognised as a very special sect of the

Jews because of its many Gentile members. Rome was familiar with the Jews' 'atheism'—their refusal to worship national and local gods as other people did—but these atheistic Christians seemed more dangerous because it was easier to join the sect; also they appealed to the outcasts of society, flouted law and order, and even prophesied the doom of Rome.

At some point the Christians were allowed to return to the capital. Paul tried to make them more respectable, giving them instructions to be 'subject to the responsible authorities, for there is no authority except from God, and those who are constituted hold their appointment from God . . .'

About 58 he made his last visit to Jerusalem, hoping to reach agreement with James on 'outstanding problems'. But he was asked to prove his orthodoxy by sponsoring four Christians taking vows in the Temple, paying their expenses and appearing with them in a state of ritual purification. He could not refuse without renouncing Judaism for good, and he was convinced that Christianity was the natural, God-willed development of Judaism. Though it meant disappointing his Gentile converts, he submitted to that demand as the lesser evil.

This satisfied James, but the Jewish authorities could not forgive Paul for the way he had disobeyed the Law in the past. He was arrested and brought before the Sanhedrin, but cleverly caused a quarrel between the Pharisees and the Sadducees, taking his stand as a Pharisee, who therefore believed in resurrection. Uproar in the Sanhedrin followed, and Lysias, commander of the Jerusalem garrison, sent him to the Procurator at Caesarea.

At the trial before Felix, Ananias the High Priest prosecuted Paul as 'a mover of rebellions among all the Jews throughout the world'. But Felix, after hearing Paul, said he must consult Lysias before giving judgment. According to *The Acts*, he tried the case again with his Jewish wife Drusilla, then kept Paul in a form of detention for two years, hoping for a bribe from the prisoner or his friends. Evidently Ananias's charge did not stick. Felix, who dealt ruthlessly with Zealots, would have given Paul the same treatment, especially when no bribe was forthcoming; he must have realised that Paul was not a political revolutionary. It is interesting, though, that no Christian testified in Paul's favour, or *The Acts* would surely have mentioned it.

The Jews renewed the charges when Felix was replaced by Festus. The new Procurator consulted King Agrippa on this embarrassing prisoner who as a Roman citizen refused to be tried at Jerusalem and had appealed to Caesar. Agrippa is reported as expressing admiration, ironical or otherwise, in the famous comment: 'Almost thou persuadest me to be a Christian.' His advice to Festus was that but for the appeal Paul could have been released; as it was, the case must be heard at Rome.

So Paul was sent off there, arrived after shipwreck and various adventures, and was again kept prisoner under easy conditions, preaching that 'the salvation of God is sent unto the Gentiles'. For two years, *The Acts* concludes, he could teach 'the things concerning the Lord Jesus Christ with all boldness, none forbidding him'. This seems to mean that he was allowed to receive frequent visitors in prison and could perhaps send sermons out for delivery by his followers to the Christian community.

Did Luke die before he had finished his narrative? That would be one explanation of the mystery: no hint as to Paul's further career or how and when he died, no suggestion that he was acquitted. For the moment he fades out of the Christian picture.

Mystery also surrounds the next important event in the Church's history. In 62, Festus died in office, and before his successor arrived (it is recorded in *Antiquities*), the High Priest Ananus summoned the court of the Sanhedrin, brought before it the brother of Jesus who was called Christ (James was his name) and certain others, and, after accusing them of breaking the Law, delivered them up to be stoned. All those in Jerusalem who were reputed to be of good sense and strict in their observance of the Law were so angry at this that they actually sent a secret report to the Emperor, begging him to restrain Ananus from his unlawful actions; some among them were even moved to go to meet the new procurator, Albinus, on his way from Alexandria, to complain especially that Ananus had no right to assemble a Sanhedrin without the Roman governor's permission.' Complaints had also been sent north to Agrippa, who promptly deposed Ananus from his office. (Ananus is not to be confused with Ananias, the High Priest who attacked Paul.)

Josephus's works contain no reference to Jesus except for this and another passage in *Antiquities*, and passages in an old Slavonic version of *The Jewish War* discovered at the beginning of this century. These last passages are made up (writes a modern historian) 'in equal parts of what now stands in the Greek [text of] Josephus, of familiar Christian traditions, and of some quite remarkable nonsense'.

Most scholars agree that they are not authentic, although one reading of a particular passage is strikingly like the account in John's Gospel of the people trying to make Jesus king against his will. So Josephus may have regarded Jesus as a healer and prophet, who called the people to repentance, refused to lead an armed revolt against Rome, but was crucified to deter his Zealot-type followers.

The other passage in *Antiquities* runs as follows: 'Now

about this time arose Jesus, a wise man, if indeed he should be called a man. For he was a doer of marvellous deeds, a teacher of men who received the truth with pleasure; and he won over to himself many Jews and many also of the Greeks. He was the Christ. And when, on the indictment of the principal men among us, Pilate had sentenced him to the cross, those who had loved him at first did not give up; for he appeared to them on the third day alive again, the divine prophets having foretold these and ten thousand other wonderful things concerning him. And even now the race of Christians, named after him, is not extinct.'

It is incredible that a non-Christian should have given such an account of Jesus, and very likely some Christian writer changed it from a previous version. Eusebius, a fourth-century bishop, is our earliest witness to the present Greek text; Origen, an Alexandrian scholar a century earlier, states categorically that Josephus did not believe Jesus was the Messiah: so Origen saw a different text from Eusebius's.

The account of James's martyrdom—although it reads as much more authentic—seems to have got altered too, for Origen also says that Josephus 'as it were, reluctantly' made that a cause of the Jewish nation's overthrow by Rome. This would be a surprising suggestion for Josephus. Possibly he saw Ananus's action as a mistake which led to a decisive breach between the richer priests and the lower clergy, turning the latter towards anti-Roman action. Or else Origen may not have had the original text either. Without these original texts, Josephus's attitude to Jesus and the Christians must remain a mystery. After the death of James, Simeon, his cousin, became leader of the Nazarenes.

In *The Jewish War* Josephus refers to an episode which also occurred in 62 on the Feast of Tabernacles: 'One Jesus, son of Ananias, a rude peasant, standing in the Temple, suddenly began to cry out, "A voice from the east, a voice from the west, a voice against Jerusalem and the Sanctuary, a voice against the bridegroom and the bride, a voice against all the people." Day after day he went about the alleys with this cry on his lips.' Arrested and beaten, he continued his cries. He was brought before Albinus, the new procurator, who had him flayed to the bone with scourges; he responded to each stroke with 'Woe to Jerusalem!' When Albinus asked him who he was, where he came from, and why he uttered these cries, the man 'answered never a word, but kept on repeating his dirge over the city, until Albinus pronounced him a maniac and let him go'.

Besides recalling the lament over Jerusalem by Jesus of Nazareth, this account of another Jesus (in Hebrew: Jehoshua, a very common name) has presumably left traces in John's Gospel. We read of Jesus crying out in the Temple during the Feast of Tabernacles and later, brought before Pilate, making no reply to the question: 'Whence art thou?'

But James did not prophesy against the Temple; he worshipped there with a devoutness acceptable to the Pharisees. Josephus, clearly prominent enough to serve on the Sanhedrin, could have been one of those who defended him— but would probably have boasted of it if he had! Not long afterwards the young Pharisee set out for Rome to intercede for the priests imprisoned by Felix.

CHAPTER 8

INTERLUDE IN ROME

Like Paul, Josephus was shipwrecked on the way to Rome. There were about six hundred on board, and they were in the sea all night. A ship from Cyrene picked up eighty survivors at dawn, including Josephus. 'Landing safely ... at Puteoli, I formed a friendship with Aliturus, an actor who was a special favourite of Nero and of Jewish origin. Through him I was introduced to Poppaea, Caesar's wife, and took the earliest opportunity of asking for her help to secure the liberation of the priests. Having besides this favour received large gifts from Poppaea, I returned to my own country.'

This is all Josephus says in his *Life* about his first visit to Rome. Once again we can only wish he had been writing an ordinary autobiography, telling us the impression made on a strict Pharisee by the capital of the Empire with its splendours and squalors, its luxury and affluence, dependent on thousands of slaves. Brutally as they were often treated, however, it was very common for a slave-owner to give his slaves freedom, sometimes on his deathbed or by testament. This meant more and more freedmen, who gained power, wealth and rank. Already by Nero's time many senators and knights were descended from slaves.

Meanwhile the Roman birth-rate continued to decline. As often happens, this was connected with luxurious living on the part of the rich and aristocratic, who instead of having children preferred to spend fantastic sums on dress, ornament, food and drink. 500 asses provided Poppaea with milk to bathe in daily, and Josephus was surely a little shocked at first by his 'God-fearing' patroness's way of life. Evidently the shock wore off.

Nero's adviser, Seneca, the Stoic philosopher, denounced luxury, and also advocated humane treatment of slaves. He had a great many himself, and was a relatively kind master. But he acquired a vast fortune through money-lending, so his emphasis on simplicity and the high moral tone of his writings leave a flavour of hypocrisy.

It was *his* brother Gallio who, as governor of Greece, refused to judge Jewish religious matters when the Jews of Corinth brought Paul to trial. Opinion turned against the ruler of the synagogue, who got beaten up. Gallio, says *The Acts*, 'cared for none of these things'. Behind the provincial governor's stern impartiality there was perhaps some sympathy for Paul, one strand in the old tradition—which is quite conceivable—that the apostle met Seneca.

By the time Josephus arrived in Rome, Seneca had retired from public life, and Burrus, his colleague as the Emperor's counsellor, was dead. The power passed to Tigellinus, corrupt and vicious, Burrus's successor as prefect of the Praetorian Guard. Readers of Tacitus would gain a false impression that from now on the Empire was falling apart; but Tacitus, great historian though he was, concentrated too much on Rome. Nero's government remained reasonably efficient in the provinces, and in 62 Roman arms had recovered from a disastrous defeat in Britain by rebel tribes under Queen Boudicca (Boadicea). The Roman governor, who was in Wales suppressing the Druids, hurried back and destroyed the British forces. Boudicca took poison, the rebellion collapsed.

In the East the buffer state of Armenia preoccupied Nero. If it was hostile, Parthia was dangerous, but attempts to conquer it stretched Roman power too far. Corbulo, a skilful general with a large army, tried—and had to make a humiliating retreat. In 64, however, he forced Tiridates, the Armenian king, to recognise Roman sovereignty, and Tiridates came to Rome the year after to receive his diadem from Nero's hands. The Emperor entertained him lavishly, partly to impress him with Rome's wealth and might— Josephus took the point as well. The settlement led to peace between Rome and Parthia for fifty years.

Nero persuaded Tiridates to be initiated into Mithraic rites. The cult of Mithras the sun-god, introduced to Rome a century earlier by captives of Pompey from Asia Minor, had become extremely powerful throughout the Empire (a Mithras temple was found in the City of London in the 1960's), and Nero was strongly attracted by it. This may partly account for his persecution of Christianity—as a dangerous rival to Mithraism.

The Emperor was by now setting the pace himself in luxury and extravagance. He also offended respectable society by going in for chariot races and performing in theatres. He sang, recited epics of his own composition, and won laurels everywhere—from judges who could scarcely be expected to show complete impartiality. Vespasian, the future Emperor, nearly lost his life for falling asleep while Nero was in full song. Josephus, no doubt, watched some of Nero's performances, and he was in Rome when the great fire broke out, which raged for nine days, reducing most of the city to ashes.

The legend of the Emperor 'fiddling' during the blaze

seems in keeping with his dramatic sense and artistic excitement, but probably has little basis in fact. It was alleged that he deliberately started the fire, but this too sounds unlikely, since he was extremely active in relief for the homeless. He also rebuilt the congested city to a much improved design, which scarcely suggests a large-scale arsonist.

He certainly made scapegoats of the Christians, however, for Tacitus bears witness to this in striking form: 'Nero found a set of profligate and abandoned wretches, who were induced to confess themselves guilty, and on the evidence of such men a number of Christians were convicted, not indeed upon clear evidence of their having set the city on fire, but rather on account of their sullen hatred of the human race. They were put to death with exquisite cruelty, and to their sufferings Nero added mockery and derision ... At length the cruelty of these proceedings filled every breast with compassion. Humanity relented in favour of the Christians ... Their crimes called for the hand of justice; but it was evident that they fell a sacrifice, not for the public good, but to appease the rage and cruelty of one man.'

Christian tradition has it that both Peter and Paul suffered martyrdom at Rome, and one of them may indeed have been among Nero's scapegoats. But if they had both been martyred in Rome at the same time, some record of this would have appeared in Church history.

After the fire, Nero built himself a magnificent palace, brought many Greek statues to Rome, and adorned his new city regardless of expense. He continued to gratify the populace with 'bread and circuses', the 'bread' part being free distributions of corn. To pay for this, for the rebuilding, and for all his extravagances, he sent his freedmen to extract more money from Italy and the provinces.

In 65 an abortive conspiracy increased his suspicions of everybody, so that he acted more tyrannically than before. He had sixteen Senators executed, and ordered others (including Seneca and Corbulo) to kill themselves. Poppaea died, and the following year he took another wife, after putting her husband to death. Treason trials started again, informers flourished, Nero's freedmen and Tigellinus asserted their powers without restraint. The Gaius story repeated itself as surviving Senators tried to buy safety by flattery of the Emperor.

In the winter of 66–67 Nero accepted an invitation from the Greek cities to visit their province. He made a spectacular progress, and formally liberated Greece, i.e. granted the cities permanent exemption from tribute. In return he was declared a god and paid all manner of honours. As actor, singer and charioteer, he appeared in the four great national games, winning (as might be guessed) all the first prizes.

Vespasian was on the Emperor's suite, forgiven apparently for his lack of artistic appreciation. The son of a knight, born in 8 A.D., Vespasian had entered the Senate. He occupied the Isle of Wight during Claudius's invasion of Britain, and became consul in 51. After this, except for a period governing the province of Africa, he had retired into private life. Now his chance came for further laurels. Reliable generals were needed, but they must not become too popular, as Corbulo had done. Vespasian, with his fairly humble origins, offered less threat to the Emperor's own power: he was the best man to settle a crisis in the east.

For soon after Josephus's return in the spring of 66, the smouldering hostility between the Jews and their Gentile neighbours and governors had blazed up into a full Jewish rebellion against the Empire. Cestius Gallus, governor of Syria, had just suffered a heavy and unexpected defeat. In February 67, Vespasian was sent out to subdue Judaea and then govern it.

Soldiers of the Praetorian Guard

CHAPTER 9

DAVID TAKES ON GOLIATH

For Josephus, anxious to show that the Jews had been intolerably provoked, Judaea's last two procurators were by far the worst. Under Albinus (62–64), Zealots secured immunity by bribery, and bands of ruffians plundered peaceable citizens, who did not dare complain to authority.

Albinus, however, appeared a paragon of virtue compared with his successor, Gessius Florus, whom Josephus accuses of driving the Jews into rebellion to divert attention from his own offences. He 'stripped whole cities, ruined entire populations, and almost proclaimed throughout the country that all were at liberty to practise brigandage, on condition that he received his share of the spoils'. The historian finished the twenty books of his *Antiquities* by asserting that it was Florus 'who compelled us to take up arms against the Romans, thinking it better to be destroyed at once than by degrees'. Tacitus, generally hostile to the Jews, gives the same verdict in his usual terse fashion: 'The Jews' patience lasted until Gessius Florus was procurator; under him the war started.'

When Cestius Gallus visited Jerusalem for the Passover in 66, 'a crowd of not less than three millions' (a record figure even for Josephus!) 'implored him to have compassion on the calamities of the nation, and denounced Florus as the ruin of the country. Florus, present at Cestius's side, scoffed at their outcry', and the Syrian governor, calming them down as best he could, returned to Antioch.

Florus soon roused the Jews' indignation once more, putting in irons twenty of their elders at Caesarea after Greek-Jewish riots there. Then he sent orders for seventeen talents to be taken from the Temple treasury in Jerusalem; at which some of the angry crowd went round begging coppers for him as if for a down-and-out. The Jews were at the time in arrears with their tribute, so Florus could claim he was within his rights. Failing to get all the money he wanted, he led an army to Jerusalem, and ordered his troops to sack the Upper Market. They looted, slaughtered men, women and children, ignored Berenice's vain appeals to Florus to stop the butchery, and would have killed her too. She managed to escape into the Herodian palace and spent the night there. Agrippa was away in Alexandria, congratulating Tiberius Alexander on his appointment as Prefect of Egypt.

Next day the 'peace party' persuaded the people to agree to a procession which was to meet and salute Florus's reinforcements coming down from Caesarea. The Roman troops, however, had been warned in advance not to respond, and at the first shouts against Florus they fell on the unarmed procession: another massacre followed. But when they tried to enter the Temple cloisters, they were pelted from the roofs and had to retreat to their camp by the palace. The rebels then cut down the Temple porticoes connecting it with the Antonia fortress. Florus returned to Caesarea, leaving an extra garrison behind. The chief priests undertook to keep order, but they and Berenice sent complaints to Cestius Gallus.

Neapolitanus, a member of his staff, came down to investigate, and met Agrippa on his way home. The people of Jerusalem gathered in force, 'begging Agrippa to rescue them, and loudly declaiming to Neapolitanus all that they had suffered from Florus'. After a tour of the ravaged city, Neapolitanus went up to the Temple: 'Here he called the multitude together, highly commended them for their loyalty to the Romans and urged them to keep the peace; then, after paying his devotions to the sanctuary of God from the permitted area' (the so-called Court of the Gentiles), he returned to Cestius.

But the people would not leave matters there. They pressed Agrippa and the chief priests to send an embassy to Nero denouncing the procurator. Knowing Nero's erratic temperament, Agrippa felt this was a dangerous gamble. He summoned the people to the gymnasium below his palace, stood on the palace roof with Berenice at his side, and made a passionate appeal to the Jewish nation to submit quietly to the power of Rome.

Josephus gives several pages to this oration, which he probably heard himself. Agrippa, who was shown a draft of *The Jewish War*, could have suggested corrections, and certainly either he or Josephus has adapted the material after the event, so that it does not read like an actual speech the King delivered at the time. For one thing, it is slightly out of context, since he was supposed to be merely advising against an embassy to Nero. Parts of the speech would also have been extremely tactless, as when he accused the Jews of 'indulging in exaggerated reproaches for minor errors'. Their interest, he declared, was to conciliate the powers that be by flattery, not to irritate them. 'There is nothing to check blows like submission, and the resignation of the wronged victim puts the wrongdoer to confusion.' A hint

The Siege of Masada. An eighteenth-century engraving.

Masada. A modern view.

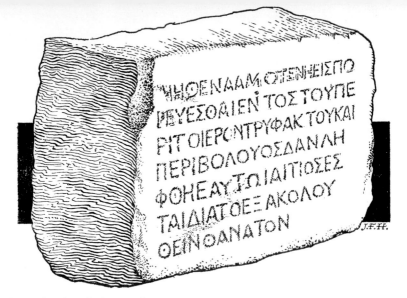

Warning inscription at the Temple in Jerusalem. Strangers might not enter on pain of death. The warning appeared in Hebrew and later in Greek as well.

A fragment of one of the Dead Sea Scrolls. This is about half the actual size.

here of the Christian precept of 'turning the other cheek'?

He recommended waiting for a new and more moderate procurator, whereas war, once started, could neither be stopped nor carried through without risk of disaster. Anyhow, the Jews had already accepted subjection for too long. They should have strained every nerve to keep out the Romans when Pompey invaded Judaea.

Agrippa reviewed the liberty-loving nations who had accepted Roman rule: 'Are you wealthier than the Gauls, stronger than the Germans, more intelligent than the Greeks, more numerous than all the peoples of the world? ... Consider what a wall of defence had the Britons, you who put your trust in the walls of Jerusalem ...; yet the Romans crossed the sea and enslaved them, and four legions now secure that vast island.' Even the Parthians, 'race of finest warriors, lords of so many nations, having so huge an army, send hostages to the Romans, and the nobility of the east may be seen in Italy ... bending to the yoke.'

The King then warned his fellow Jews against counting on divine assistance. The Roman Empire could never have been built up without God's aid, and anyhow the Jews could neither in wartime keep God's commandments, like obedience to the Sabbath, nor call for His help when disobeying them. He pointed also to the peril threatening Jews in foreign cities, 'for there is not a people in the world which does not contain some of our race. All these, if you go to war, will be butchered by your adversaries, and through the follies of a handful of men every city will be drenched with Jewish blood.'

In his peroration he told his listeners to take pity on their mother city and its sacred precincts: 'Spare the temple and preserve for yourselves the sanctuary with its holy places ... If you make the right decision, you will enjoy with me the blessings of peace; but if you let yourselves be carried away by your passion, you will face, without me, this tremendous danger.' 'The blessings of peace' sounds almost an afterthought: basically the Jews had to submit because might was right.

Perhaps this was a realistic assessment, however shameful to modern ears and to many Jews at the time. In the terrible dilemma presented throughout history to weaker nations, tribes and groups, is it more discreditable to endure persecution and injustice as best you can than to start violent resistance against hopeless odds and probably widen the area of suffering? Opinions will always be divided on this, as on the hopelessness of the odds. For ever since David slew Goliath, the Jewish people had trusted in the Lord to protect His own. Many would go on expecting this, whatever the peace party might say.

After his speech Agrippa burst into tears, as did Berenice. His audience protested that they were taking up arms against Florus, not the Romans. He told them they had already rebelled by cutting down the porticoes and falling into arrears with their tribute. For the moment this was accepted: rebuilding of the porticoes began, the Sanhedrin members collected tribute in the surrounding villages and soon made up the arrears of forty talents.

But later, when Agrippa tried to make the people agree to obey Florus until a replacement was sent, 'they heaped abuse on him and formally proclaimed his banishment from the city; some even dared to throw stones at him'. Agrippa prudently withdrew to his own dominions: the revolutionaries were now clearly out of control. Soon the first real acts of war against Rome took place.

First a band of Zealots, led by Menahem, a son of Judas of Galilee, attacked the Herodian fortress of Masada, took it by a stratagem (Josephus gives no details), killed the Roman garrison and installed a Jewish one. Menahem now had a vast store of arms, an essential condition for launching the great war of liberation.

About the same time, early in August 66, a symbolic declaration of war took place in Jerusalem, when 'Eleazar, son of Ananias the High Priest, a very daring youth ... persuaded those who officiated in the Temple services to accept no gift of sacrifices from a foreigner'. This meant refusing sacrifice (and prayers) on behalf of the Emperor, long recognised as a Jewish substitute for the oath of loyalty. From other contexts also we see that most of the younger generation were the fiercest advocates of rebellion. Religious and patriotic fervour were linked in a bitter hatred of Rome.

Appeals to call off the sacrifice ban fell on deaf ears: the rebels had the full support of the lower clergy, perhaps also of the Nazarenes. The peace party withdrew to the upper city, leaving Eleazar in control of the Temple. They sent urgent calls for help to Florus, who inexplicably took no action, and to Agrippa, who sent down a wing of cavalry from his territories. After a week's savage fighting, the rebels forced an evacuation of the upper city, set fire to the High Priest's house, the palaces of Agrippa and Berenice, and the public archives, 'eager to destroy the money-lenders' bonds and prevent the recovery of debts, in order to win over a host of grateful debtors and to cause a rising of the poor against the rich'.

Next day they captured the Antonia, burned it down and killed the garrison. Then they turned their attention to the complex known as Herod's palace. Agrippa's men and some of the peace party, including Josephus, had escaped to this, and were holding it with another Roman garrison. The

95

rebels were at first less successful here, but after Menahem arrived from Masada and took over the siege, the defenders lost heart and asked to be allowed to leave the fortress under safe conduct. Menahem granted this only to Agrippa's forces and his fellow Jews; the Romans retreated to the palace's three high towers. Menahem's followers rushed in, and killed the stragglers. Next day they caught and killed Ananias.

Eleazar was indignant at his father's murder, and a private war began between the victorious rebel leaders. Menahem had Messianic claims, recognised at Masada; in Jerusalem his enemies called him an insufferable tyrant. When he entered the Temple in state, wearing the robes of a king, to pay his devotions, Eleazar's men rushed on him and his bodyguard, who offered a brief resistance, then fled. Everyone caught was massacred, a hunt was made for those in hiding. Menahem himself was dragged into the open, tortured and killed. A few managed to escape to Masada, including a cousin of Menahem's, who later became leader of the fortress defenders.

The Roman garrison in their three towers saw that their position was hopeless. Metilius the commander offered to surrender with all their arms and belongings in return for a safe conduct. The offer was accepted, oaths exchanged, Metilius led his men out, and they laid down their arms. 'Eleazar's party fell on them', writes Josephus, 'surrounded and massacred them; the Romans neither resisting nor suing for mercy, but merely appealing with loud cries to "the covenant" and "the oaths". So perished all save Metilius, who saved his life by entreaties and promises to turn Jew and even be circumcised.' To add to the heinousness of this crime, Josephus comments, it took place on the Sabbath, 'a day on which Jews ... abstain even from the most innocent acts'. Many patriotic Jews were horrified both by the treachery and by the prospect of retribution.

Agrippa's warning about the fate of Jews everywhere was soon justified, starting with a massacre of Caesarea's entire Jewish population which, Josephus says, occurred 'the same day and the same hour, as it were by the hand of providence'. Twenty thousand were slaughtered in an hour (his figures again). The whole country responded by savage reprisals: parties of Jews sacked Syrian villages and the Greek cities known as the Decapolis. The inevitable chain reaction continued, as the Gentiles in other cities rose against their Jewish inhabitants all over Syria.

In Alexandria, when the Jews tried to take revenge for Gentile attacks, Tiberius Alexander, the new Prefect, quelled them with the two Roman legions stationed there plus auxiliaries from Libya. The troops were given permission to kill the rioters, plunder their property, and burn down their houses. They rushed to the Jewish quarter, and after fierce Jewish resistance a wholesale slaughter took place. When Tiberius called them off, the Gentile population went on with the killing and looting.

About this time the Jewish rebels captured the Herodian fort of Machaerus on the north-east of the Dead Sea, where John the Baptist had been imprisoned and beheaded. The Romans evacuated it under treaty, and they installed their own garrison. All Judaea and Peraea was for the moment in Jewish hands.

Meanwhile Cestius Gallus had at last moved south with the twelfth legion, 6000 men from the other three Syrian legions, and troops supplied by Agrippa and two other puppet kings. Quickly regaining control of Galilee, he hurried down towards Jerusalem—it was mid-October, the rains would soon make the roads impassable—and camped six miles outside the Jewish capital. The Jews were celebrating the Feast of Tabernacles, but abandoned it, rushed to arms, and broke through the enemy's lines, killing over five hundred. Their onslaught was at last checked, but a man called Simon Ben Gioras fell on the rearguard of the retreating Romans and carried off many baggage mules. Cestius stayed three days in his former quarters, while Jewish rebels occupied the mountains round Jerusalem.

Bringing up his whole force, he routed them, pursued them to Jerusalem, and pitched his camp on Mount Scopus, a hill on the north-east. When he led troops into the suburbs, the rebels retired to the inner city and the Temple, and Cestius pressed on to a position opposite the walls of the upper palace. If he had decided there and then to force his way through the walls, Josephus asserts, he would have captured the city and the war would have been over: 'But his camp prefect, with most of the cavalry commanders, bribed by Florus, diverted him from the attempt.' Once more, very unconvincingly, Florus gets the blame: even if the bribes had been offered and accepted, which seems unlikely, Cestius would not have listened to his staff's advice without strong arguments for delay. What the arguments were, remains a mystery.

He missed another chance when some of the priests contacted him with a promise to open the gates. He ignored these overtures, suspecting a trap, and the rebels pulled the peacemongers down from the wall, stoned them and drove them into their houses. Then they kept up a running fire to stop the Romans scaling the wall. After five days of vain attempts, Cestius sent a large force to attack the north side of the Temple. The defenders eventually gave way, and a band of legionaries, forming a *testudo* (shields linked over their heads, like the shell of a giant tortoise), got over the wall, and prepared to set fire to the Temple gate.

'A terrible panic now seized the rebels, many of whom were already slinking out of the city in the belief that it was on the verge of capture. The people took heart again' —Josephus, in this context, being one of 'the people'—'and the more the vile wretches gave ground, the nearer did the people advance to the gates, to open them and welcome Cestius as a benefactor. Had he but carried on for a while with the siege, he would have taken the city then and there; but God, I suppose, because of those wretches, had already turned away even from His sanctuary and ordained that that day should not see the end of the war.

'At any rate, Cestius, realising neither the despair of the besieged nor the real mood of the people, suddenly recalled his troops, gave up his hopes, without having suffered any defeat, and . . . retired from the city.' Unless some dramatic historical discovery is made, we shall never know why Cestius turned away. Had he taken Jerusalem that October day in 66, it would have changed the course of history.

Greatly encouraged, the rebels attacked the Roman rear-guard, killing large numbers. After spending the night at Scopus, Cestius continued his retreat, which soon became a rout; only nightfall saved the Romans from being completely destroyed. The day after that, having pursued the mauled army some way further, the rebels 'turned and carried off the machines, plundered the corpses, collected the booty left on the route, and with songs of triumph retraced their steps to the capital'. Jewish casualties were few, while the Romans and their allies had lost over 5000 infantry and nearly 500 cavalry.

So God had shown His hand again. Goliath was in utter confusion, and the first round had gone to David. But Rome's giant power could not be toppled by one defeat, as many Jews realised. Anticipating Roman vengeance, they escaped and joined Cestius, who sent some of them off to report to Nero in Greece: they were to blame Florus, now dead, for the war, thus reducing the risk to Cestius. He was in fact allowed to remain at his post, while Vespasian dealt with the Jews.

In Jerusalem, the triumphant rebels 'brought over to their side such pro-Romans as still remained'—Josephus among them. Ananus, the former High Priest, was one of two men elected to govern Jerusalem. Another Eleazar, who had led the pursuit of Cestius, now held the Roman spoils and much of the public treasure. He behaved arrogantly and at first was not given special office. But his intrigues and newly acquired wealth gradually won him power, says Josephus, and in the end the people made him supreme commander. This Eleazar (son of Simon) remained a rebel leader throughout the war. Nothing more is heard, however, of Eleazar the High Priest's son, whose men had killed Menahem.

The country was divided into six districts, with generals or governors appointed for each. One of these was Josephus, who had the district of Galilee assigned to him.

The young Pharisee's 'finest hour' had struck.

Coin of Simon and Eleazar (A.D. 66)

CHAPTER 10

GENERAL JOSEPHUS

For a few months Josephus himself is the chief character in *The Jewish War*, and what happened in Galilee while he was governor and general receives a great deal of space. But he is as unreliable as ever on his own behaviour, and to confuse things still more, a parallel account in the *Life* often contradicts his earlier version, for instance on why he was appointed in the first place.

One of his rivals at that time was a man called Justus from Tiberias, and much later Justus wrote a history (none of it has survived) which accused Josephus of responsibility for the rebellion in Galilee. The *Life* is a counter-attack, and Josephus shows easily enough that Justus and his fellow-citizens were already in revolt. But his defence line is ambiguous:

'After the defeat of Cestius the leading men in Jerusalem, aware that the bandits and revolutionaries had no lack of weapons, were afraid that ... they might be powerless to resist their opponents ... So when they learnt that not all Galilee had yet revolted from the Romans ... they sent me with two other priests of the highest character ... to persuade the ill-intentioned people to lay down their arms and that it was better for these to be left in the hands of the best qualified members of the nation. They ... should have their weapons in constant readiness ..., waiting meanwhile to see what the Romans would do.'

In other words, 'moderates' like Josephus were as much afraid of the Zealots as of Rome, and perhaps hoped for a chance to come to terms with the Romans.

Still, *The Jewish War* gives the impression of a governor planning vigorously for an independent Galilee: 'As for Josephus'—throughout the book he speaks of himself in the third person—'he made it his first care to win the affection of the inhabitants.' He appointed seventy magistrates for the whole country and seven local officials for each city. Then he fortified the main cities, though 'John, son of Levi, fortified Gischala* at his own expense, on the instruction of Josephus'. This is the first appearance in Josephus's history of the man who became his great enemy.

The new governor also levied a large army of young men, and set about organising and training them along Roman lines. He issued stern 'conduct directives' and said he would note 'whether they abstained from their habitual crimes, theft and looting, and stopped defrauding their countrymen and regarding as personal profit an injury sustained by their most intimate friends'. A pretty vicious lot, the Galileans, by the sound of it.

John began to intrigue against Josephus, spreading reports that he was intending to betray the country; and soon there was an opportunity to make the charge stick. The garrison of a village, having robbed Agrippa's steward of all his money and baggage, took their booty to Josephus, then at the city of Tarichaeae, who handed it over to a leading

* Gischala is now the village of Jish. Josephus started a road to its well, which Edwin Samuel—a district commissioner of Galilee under the British Mandate—'was proud to have completed nineteen hundred years later.'
(Edwin Samuel, A LIFETIME IN JERUSALEM, Valentine, Mitchell, 1970)

citizen for safe-keeping and eventual return. The garrison denounced Josephus as a traitor, and an army was raised in the neighbouring cities to attack him. A mob urged on by John gathered in the hippodrome at Tarichaeae, clamouring for him to be stoned or burnt alive. His friends and body-guard fled, but the undaunted governor 'rushed out with clothes torn and ashes sprinkled on his head, his hands behind his back and his sword hung from his neck'.

After this theatrical entry, he got the people of Tarichaeae on his side by asserting that he had kept the money for the fortifying of their city, because he feared that 'the people of Tiberias and of the other cities had their eyes on these spoils'. Sections of the mob were soon at each other's throats, and the majority withdrew, but two thousand armed men made a rush at Josephus, who escaped back to his house, hotly pursued.

He now carried out a second ruse, which he recounts with pride rather than shame. Mounting to the roof, he silenced them by a gesture of his hand, and said that with all the shouting he had no idea what they wanted; so they had better send a deputation in and he would fall in with all their demands. The deputation was in the house a long time, and the crowd thought they were still negotiating. But the governor's staff had been giving them a terrible whipping, flaying them to the bone. 'Suddenly Josephus had the doors thrown open and the men dismissed, all covered with blood, a spectacle which struck such terror into his enemies that they dropped their arms and fled.'

John tried a new plot in Tiberias, and sent soldiers to kill Josephus while he was addressing a large crowd in the stadium, on a hillock right by the lake. 'As the men drew their swords, people shouted, and Josephus turned round to see the blade at his throat. He leapt down on to the beach, jumped into a boat, and escaped to the middle of the lake.' His soldiers attacked the conspirators, but in contrast to his brutality at Tarichaeae, Josephus sent instructions 'to kill nobody and call none of the culprits to account'. John fled back to Gischala, and even when Galileans came protesting their loyalty and demanding John's punishment, Josephus 'thanked them for their goodwill but checked their impetuosity, preferring to overcome his enemies by diplomacy rather than slaughter'.

He issued a proclamation, however, threatening to seize the property and burn the houses of all those of John's supporters in each city who did not abandon him within five days. Three thousand surrendered, but John was safe at Gischala and sent messengers to Jerusalem denouncing Josephus as a tyrant. Josephus had plenty of enemies at Jerusalem as well; they got a decree passed recalling him from his command. A force of 2500 men set out for Galilee to back this decree, and three cities went over to its leaders. Somehow he reclaimed the cities, got the leaders into his power by stratagem, and sent them back to Jerusalem—where they apparently faced indignant citizens and had to flee for their lives.

A few days later Tiberias, one of the disaffected cities, revolted again, appealing to Agrippa for help. Josephus sailed at once for Tiberias with all the boats he could find in the lake—but with only four sailors on board each. Imagining at a distance that they were all filled with troops, the conspirators threw down their arms, waved olive branches and implored him to spare the city. Another 'stratagem' followed, so improbable that he would hardly have invented it.

After bitter reproaches he offered to receive deputies who would help him secure the town. Ten leading citizens responded, then fifty more, and so on until the six hundred elders of the town were in boats. The skippers had orders to sail back to Tarichaeae and shut the elders in prison. Of those left, the chief conspirator Clitus was to have his hands cuts off, but begged for one hand to be spared. When the governor consented, Clitus drew his sword and cut off his own left hand.

This did not stop further revolts, however, by Tiberias and also Sepphoris. After suppressing these, he delivered the two cities over to his soldiers to plunder, then collected the spoils and restored them to the people 'to regain their affection'. It seems an unlikely way to achieve that end, and cannot have much pleased the soldiers. In any case, Sepphoris admitted a pro-Roman garrison soon afterwards; but most of Galilee remained more or less under the governor's control.

Meanwhile the situation in Jerusalem, during that winter of 66–67, was still very fluid. 'Ananus the High Priest and all the leading men who were not pro-Roman busied themselves with repair of the walls and the collection of engines of war. In every quarter of the city missiles and suits of armour were being forged; masses of young men were undergoing a desultory training; and the whole scene was one of tumult ... The dejection of the moderates was profound ... The city before the coming of the Romans wore the appearance of a place doomed to destruction. Ananus, nevertheless, had the hope of gradually abandoning these warlike preparations and making the discontented elements and the mad so-called Zealots adopt a more sensible policy.' Ananus, like Josephus, was trying to keep all options open.

He sent a force to put down the Zealot chief Simon, who had collected a private army to plunder and kill the wealthy. Simon escaped to Masada, and from here raided the countryside of Idumaea. To protect it, the local magistrates raised an army and garrisoned the villages. The Jewish civil war, already in full swing, was to continue all through the war against the Romans.

The first engagements with Roman troops since the defeat of Cestius taught the Jews that high enthusiasm was not enough against a well-disciplined force. They made two attacks on the Gentile city of Ascalon, on the coast south west of Jerusalem. The garrison was small, but both times its commander routed the attackers, killing thousands.

After a brief switch to the capital and Nero's appointment of Vespasian, Josephus's history returns to Galilee. When Vespasian arrived in Syria, he received a deputation from pro-Roman Sepphoris, asking for protection. As it was the largest town in Galilee and very strongly fortified, he chose it as a base for his whole campaign. From here a large force overran the surrounding country, laying waste the plains, pillaging property, killing all able-bodied men: 'Galilee from end to end became a scene of fire and blood; from no misery was it exempt. The one refuge for the hunted inhabitants was in the cities fortified by Josephus.'

Titus, Vespasian's elder son, brought up the fifteenth legion from Alexandria, and contingents joined Vespasian from Agrippa and three other puppet kings: with the two Syrian legions and additional forces, the army amounted to nearly 50,000 men. The defenders of Jotapata, another large city, burst out on the Roman troops who were about to attack it, and routed them. But when Vespasian moved south with his immense army, the soldiers under Josephus's command dispersed and fled. Josephus took refuge in Tiberias, and sent express messengers to Jerusalem asking if the magistrates intended to negotiate. If so, they should tell him at once; if not, they should send him a force capable of coping with the Romans. We do not hear what they answered. The second alternative was impossible, but no authority came for negotiations.

Vespasian captured and burned the town of Gabara, and killed all adult males, 'the Romans showing no mercy to young or old, so bitter was their hatred of the nation and their memory of what had been done to Cestius.' He then burnt all the villages and towns in the neighbourhood. Some were already deserted, in the others he took the inhabitants as slaves.

Then he made plans to deal with Jotapata, at which 'Josephus hurriedly left Tiberias and entered Jotapata, his arrival raising the Jews' low spirits. A deserter brought Vespasian the welcome news of the general's movement, and urged him to attack the city quickly, because its fall, if he could only capture Josephus, would amount to the capture of all Judaea.'

Such self-glorification is so normal for our historian that it almost ceases to be surprising. Vespasian, he goes on to say, thought it a godsend that the man 'reputed to be the cleverest of his enemies, had thus deliberately entered a prison'. The whole army invested the city. It was early June in 67.

Perched on a cliff, with deep valleys on three sides, Jotapata had strong natural defences besides the walls Josephus had built. Vespasian decided that a full siege would be necessary, and began building huge earthworks. These, however, were at first demolished by Jewish raiding parties. Closing up his troops, Vespasian managed to raise an embankment till it was almost level with the walls; but Josephus, finding a way of protecting *his* builders, increased the height of the walls to thirty feet with many towers and a sturdy parapet at the top. The Romans were 'greatly disheartened; the ingenuity of Josephus and the inhabitants' perseverance astounded them'. Vespasian now began a blockade to starve the city into surrender.

Water was the chief shortage for the besieged, and Josephus rationed it; the Romans attacked the places where the water ration was being distributed. The ingenious governor had dripping garments hung round the battlements, so that the whole wall was suddenly streaming with water; the enemy must be led to believe they had more than enough to drink. He also found a ravine, neglected by the Roman outposts, through which new food supplies could be brought in—but eventually this gap in the blockade was stopped. With both food and water failing, Josephus felt it was time for him to make his escape.

As he was discussing flight with the principal citizens, the people 'crowded around him, imploring him not to abandon them, as they depended on him alone ... Children, old men, women with infants in their arms, all threw themselves weeping before him; they embraced and held him by his feet, they implored him with sobs to stay and share their fortune ... With Josephus on the spot, they were convinced no disaster could befall them.'

Much moved—and also guessing he would be watched—he decided to remain; and (if we can credit his own account) showed personal heroism. 'Now is the time,' he exclaimed, 'to begin the combat, when all hope of deliverance is past. It is a fine thing to sacrifice life for renown and by some glorious exploit to ensure in falling the memory of posterity.' With these words 'he sallied out with his bravest warriors, dispersed the guards and, penetrating to the Romans' camp, tore up the tents of skin under which they were sheltered on the embankment, and set fire to the works. This he repeated the next day . . . and for a series of days and nights tirelessly continued the fight.'

When Vespasian brought his battering ram into action, Josephus lowered sacks filled with chaff to deaden its blows. The Romans cut the cords supporting the sacks. Still the Jews were not beaten. Several times they made charges out of the city with all the dry wood they could find, and set fire to the enemy's engines, wicker shelters, and earthworks. But in the end they had to give ground, defeated especially by missiles from the Roman engines; Josephus says there was a man standing near him whose head was carried off by a stone, to land 600 yards away as if shot by a sling.

Vespasian assembled picked troops opposite breaches which the ram had made in the wall, while others went up the scaling ladders at the intact parts to draw off the defenders. A fierce battle followed, and Josephus had the women shut up in their houses, so that their wailing should not lower the combatants' morale. When the Roman vanguard were mounting the ramparts with their *testudo* of locked shields, Josephus first had boiling oil poured on to them, which ran down inside their armour, causing terrible agony, and then poured boiled clover over the gangway planks so that the attackers slipped and fell on to the earthworks or were crushed under foot. Towards evening, after severe losses, Vespasian called off his troops.

But the devices of Roman siegecraft were not yet exhausted. Three fifty-foot towers, covered with sheet-iron, were erected on the earthworks, and the artillery protected by the towers now had easy targets, so that the defenders were at last driven from the wall. The fall of Jotapata could only be a matter of time.

On the 47th day of the siege, in the last week of July, a deserter reported that the city could be captured if the

Romans went in just before dawn when the weary sentries generally snatched some sleep. Vespasian was suspicious, for a prisoner taken earlier had held out under torture, refusing to betray anything about the state of the town, and 'was finally crucified, meeting death with a smile'—we are reminded of Josephus's tribute to the Essenes' endurance of torture. Still, the deserter's report sounded plausible, and the attack before dawn was worth trying.

The Roman army advanced in silence to the walls. Titus with a few men mounted them first, cut down the sentries and entered the city. The rest of the army followed, took the citadel, and were ranging through the streets in broad daylight before the inhabitants knew what had happened. The Romans gave no quarter, and 'thrust the people down the steep slope from the citadel in a general massacre'. Many Jews committed suicide, defence was impossible. The slaughter continued all that day and the next day, as the Romans searched the underground vaults and caves. They killed everyone they found except for women, small children, and twelve hundred whom they took prisoner. The total number of Jewish dead through the siege and at its terrible end is given by Josephus as forty thousand. Vespasian had the city rased to the ground.

The next few days produced the turning-point in Josephus's life, and it is sad that his account of its first climax should kill all respect for his character; he describes his horrible behaviour with an extraordinary mixture of smug vanity and shameless exposure of his moral blindness.

'Aided by some divine providence,' he escaped just before the city was taken, plunging into a deep pit which led to a cave. Here—he found forty others in hiding, with enough food to last for some time. After he had been in the cave for two days, their hiding-place was discovered, and

Vespasian sent two tribunes offering to spare Josephus's life if he came up. Josephus was too frightened of Roman treachery and punishment to accept, but then Vespasian sent a third tribune called Nicanor, who was a friend of Josephus's and persuaded him that Vespasian's offer could be trusted. While he was hesitating, the soldiers tried to set fire to the cave, but Vespasian stopped them, anxious to take the Jewish general alive.

Then Josephus, a skilled interpreter of dreams, familiar with the Jewish sacred books, suddenly 'saw' what their prophecies and his recent dreams had meant. He offered up a silent prayer to God: 'Since it pleases Thee, who didst create the Jewish nation, to break Thy work, since fortune has wholly passed to the Romans, and since Thou hast made choice of my spirit to announce the things that are to come, I willingly surrender to the Romans and consent to live; but I take Thee to witness that I go not as a traitor but as Thy minister.'

The Jews who shared his retreat saw things in a very different light, and threatened to kill him if he surrendered; they proposed joint suicide as the only honourable course. He proceeded to lecture them on suicide as a sin against God and nature—an eloquent philosophical discourse which in fact he would scarcely have delivered with their swords at his throat.

'But he, addressing one by name, fixing his general's eye of command upon another, clasping the hand of a third, shaming a fourth by entreaty ... succeeded in warding off the blades of all, turning like a wild beast surrounded by hunters to face his successive attackers. Even in his extremity, they still held their general in reverence; their hands were powerless, their swords glanced aside, and many, in the act of thrusting at him, dropped their weapons of their own accord.

'Even then, his resource did not forsake him. Trusting God's protection, he put his life to the hazard, and said: "Since we are resolved to die, come, let us leave the lot to decide the order in which we are to kill ourselves; let him who draws the first lot fall by the hand of him who comes next; fortune will thus take her course through the whole number, and we shall be spared from taking our lives with our own hands. For it would be unjust that, when the rest were gone, any should repent and escape." '

This was accepted, they all drew lots, and each man 'presented his throat to his neighbour, in the assurance that his general was forthwith to share his fate; for sweeter to them than life was the thought of death with Josephus. He, however, (should one say by fortune or by the providence of God?) was left alone with one other; and, anxious neither to be condemned by the lot nor, should he be left to the last, to stain his hand with the blood of a fellow-countryman, he persuaded this man also, under a pledge, to remain alive.'

Instead of the words in brackets, the Slavonic version of *The Jewish War* has: 'He counted the numbers with cunning and thereby misled them all'—which is more honest and more credible, though it is still remarkable that the others let themselves be taken in. Few confidence tricks, including the efficient rigging of the lot, can have been so difficult to perform. Doubtless the other 'last man' was in it too. Josephus does not give his name, nor do we know if the pledge was honoured; more likely some way was found of getting rid of this solitary witness.

'Having thus survived both the war with the Romans and that with his own friends, Josephus was brought by Nicanor into Vespasian's presence. The Romans all flocked to see him', and many were thirsting for his blood. But Titus 'was specially touched by the fortitude of Josephus under misfortune and by pity for his youth': Josephus was now thirty, four years older than Titus, so the comment is strange. At any rate, Titus 'brought over many Romans to share his pity for Josephus, and his pleading with his father was the main influence in saving the prisoner's life. Vespasian, however, ordered him to be guarded with every precaution, intending shortly to send him to Nero.'

On hearing this, Josephus asked for, and obtained, a private audience with the general. The only others present were Titus and two friends, and the prisoner talked to Vespasian in these terms:— 'You imagine, Vespasian, that in the person of Josephus you have taken a mere captive; but I come to you as a messenger of greater destinies. Had I not been sent on this errand by God, I knew the law of the Jews and how it becomes a general to die. Are you sending me to Nero? Why do that? Do you think that Nero and those who before your accession succeed him, will continue in power? You will be Caesar, Vespasian, you will be Emperor, you and your son here. Bind me then yet more securely in chains and keep me for yourself; for you, Caesar, are master not of me only, but of land and sea and the whole human race. For myself, I ask to be punished with stricter custody, if I have dared to trifle with the words of God.'

An 'inspired guess' in the modern sense, or a truly inspired prediction: who knows? Did he really make it anyhow? Probably he did, for his name is given elsewhere in this connection, so the prophecy may have been in Vespasian's Memoirs. It is attributed in the tradition of the Rabbis to Johanan Ben Zakkai, then leader of Hillel's disciples, who foretold the Temple's destruction as well long before the event. Despite conspiracies Nero's throne still seemed firm enough, nor was Vespasian first candidate for a new emperor. Even so, revolution was perhaps in the air, and he was impressed to find other prisoners confirming Josephus's claim that he had foretold the capture of Jotapata after a siege of forty-seven days.

Less sceptical now, Vespasian did not release the prophet but 'presented him with fine clothes and other precious gifts, and continued to treat him with kindness and consideration, being warmly supported by Titus in these courtesies'. According to the *Life*, the gifts included a wife, one of the women taken prisoner at Caesarea; they were together only two years. All Josephus says is: 'She left me on my obtaining my release and accompanying Vespasian to Alexandria. There I married again.'

After the fall of Jotapata, Vespasian withdrew his army to Caesarea, where they were enthusiastically received, chiefly out of hatred for the Jews; he had to quell the crowd's demands for Josephus's punishment.

Meanwhile, the news from Galilee trickled through to Jerusalem, and Josephus was reported dead. This, he says, caused general lamentation. While individuals mourned for their near and dear, 'all alike wept for Josephus'. But when it became known that he was alive, in Roman hands, and receiving specially favourable treatment, 'the demonstrations of anger were as loud as the former expressions of affection when he was believed dead. Some abused him as a coward, others as a traitor . . . and curses were heaped upon his devoted head. The citizens . . . were now animated with greater fury against the Romans by the thought that, in having their revenge on them, they would also be avenged on Josephus. Such was the state of agitation prevailing in Jerusalem.'

Poor Josephus! It makes a grim epilogue to his few months as a patriot general. Having rendered unto Caesar the things which were Caesar's, and perhaps other things besides, he was consistently loyal to his new masters for the rest of his life—for which he had his reward. But in his native land most Jews considered him a renegade and a traitor; they still do so today.

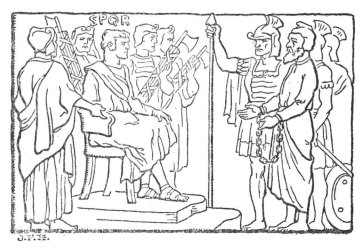

A Roman Judgment

CHAPTER 11

CIVIL WARS, JEWISH AND ROMAN

Jotapata's fall left several other rebel strongholds, but by mid-November Vespasian had completed the 'mopping up' and was in firm control of all Galilee. John of Gischala escaped to Jerusalem, and began playing a prominent part in the civil war there, which went on fiercely all through the winter and the spring of 68.

It was basically a struggle between a peace party, which hoped for a chance to negotiate with the Romans, and the Zealots, who were powerful enough to kill many of their enemies and seize the Temple as a fortress. To the horror of the old 'establishment', they had the High Priest chosen by lot. The peasant who had drawn it was brought to Jerusalem and dressed up for his assumed part. 'They put the sacred vestments on him and instructed him how to act . . . The other priests, watching from a distance this mockery of their law, could not keep back their tears.'

The priests' leaders were Ananus and Jesus, son of Gamalus. Ananus was the High Priest who had James martyred, and if Josephus disapproved of his action then, he has nothing but praise for him here. Summoning the people to a general assembly, Ananus delivered a stirring appeal to them to rise against the Zealots, claiming that even if they fell beneath Roman arms, which God forbid, 'we can suffer no greater cruelty than these men have already inflicted upon us'. The 'people' responded, and drove the Zealots from the Temple's outer court into the shrine itself. Ananus had six thousand armed men guard the porticoes.

He was unwise enough to trust as intermediary the crafty John of Gischala, who promptly told the Zealot leaders that Ananus meant to betray the city to the Romans. At John's suggestion a delegation went south to call in the Idumaeans, a 'turbulent and disorderly people who only needed a little flattery from their suitors', says Josephus, 'to seize their arms and rush into a battle as to a feast.' Twenty thousand of them marched on Jerusalem.

That night they camped outside the walls. There was a terrific storm, and Ananus failed to inspect his sentries outside the Temple: not through negligence, Josephus claims, but because Destiny willed it, as she also lulled some of the sentries to sleep. Aided by the wind and thunder, a small party of Zealots sawed through the bars of the Temple gates, did the same with the city gate opposite the Idumaeans, and let their allies in. The Idumaeans first freed the remaining Zealots in the Temple, then fell on the guards. Having overcome resistance in the Temple area, the victors went on the rampage, slaughtering everyone in sight. They hunted out Ananus and Jesus, killed them, and left the corpses to be eaten by dogs.

Josephus does not find many of his fellow Jews to praise, but Ananus receives a superb 'obituary' which makes him sound most untypical of the chief priests of the time. The fall of the Jewish state, the historian writes, began on the day when the Jews saw 'the captain of their salvation butchered in the heart of Jerusalem. A man on every ground revered and of the highest integrity ... Ananus delighted to treat the very humblest as his equals. Unique in his love of liberty and an enthusiast for democracy, he always put the public welfare above his private interests. To maintain peace was his supreme object. He knew that Roman power was irresistible, but, when driven to provide for a state of war, he tried to make sure that, if the Jews did not come to terms, the struggle should at least be skilfully conducted. In a word, had Ananus lived ... they would undoubtedly either have arranged terms ... or else have greatly delayed the Romans' victory under such a general.'

Clearly Josephus's lost hero was more interested in the former alternative, and the historian may be right in his judgment: this was perhaps the last time a 'peace party' leader could hope to carry the people with him. If he had succeeded in suing for terms then, it might have saved the Jews from final disaster: one of the great 'ifs' of history.

Idumaeans and Zealots continued their slaughter for some time, crushing all opposition and making the high-born their special target. Eventually the Idumaeans were persuaded by one of the Zealots to leave the city. Before doing so, they liberated two thousand men in prison, who at once fled to Masada and joined Simon there. During the Passover, Simon and his men raided and captured a small town called En-geddi. They followed this up by similar raids around the Masada area, and were 'joined daily by many licentious recruits from every quarter'.

The departure of the Idumaeans did not stop the Zealots' reign of terror in Jerusalem. They arrested thousands; every charge, however trivial, was punishable by death, and 'none escaped save those whose humble birth put them utterly beneath notice, unless by accident'. Large numbers tried to flee to the Romans, and the rich successfully bribed the guards, while the poor were caught and slaughtered. At one point John of Gischala tried to achieve supreme power, but this led to a split in the Zealot camp, which made the lives of the ordinary people still more precarious.

Vespasian's staff had urged him to attack Jerusalem while the Jews were fighting each other. But he decided that if he did so, it would only unite them again. During the spring, however, his chief lieutenant succeeded in occupying Peraea as far south as the fortress of Machaerus, which remained in Jewish hands.

News had by now come through of a revolt in Gaul under the Roman prefect Vindex. It made Vespasian anxious to conclude the Palestine campaign quickly, so as to be ready for any trouble in other parts of the Empire. He marched south, and easily gained control of the rest of Judaea and northern Idumaea, laying waste the country he passed through. At the end of June he entered Jericho, from which most of the inhabitants had fled. After establishing camps there and at another town, he returned to Caesarea and prepared for the onslaught on Jerusalem. But just at this point the Jews gained an unexpected breathing-space. For further news arrived from Rome itself: Nero was dead, the Empire had a new ruler.

On his return from his acclamation in Greece, Nero had ignored the growing discontent which had spread in widening circles from the capital. Vindex's revolt was crushed by a loyal general, its leader killed; but it had involved Galba, an elderly aristocrat, governor of Spain. Having burnt his boats, Galba could only go over to the attack, so the Spanish as well as the Gallic legions deserted Nero, followed by the Praetorian Guard. The Senate declared Nero a public enemy, he fled to the suburbs and there killed himself after the celebrated last words: '*Qualis artifex pereo!*', 'What an artist perishes in me!'

Demands for the restoration of the republic were quickly muffled. That was not what the legions wanted, and they held a controlling interest. For, as Tacitus commented, 'the secret of empire was out, that an emperor could be made elsewhere than at Rome'.

Galba was proclaimed Emperor by the Senate, but unwisely took his time leading the Spanish army to Rome. Then he refused to give the Praetorian Guard the lavish pay bonus they had come to expect. Besides gaining a reputation for meanness, he made a bitter enemy of Otho, Poppaea's ex-husband, by passing him over as deputy. Otho bribed the Praetorians; and in mid-January 69 they lynched Galba in the forum and forced Otho on the Senate as the new ruler. Galba earned a famous epitaph from Tacitus: 'By general consent a good man for emperor—if only he hadn't been one.'

Even before Galba's death the legions in Germany were hailing their commander, Aulus Vitellius, as Emperor. He led them in a two-pronged invasion of Italy, and his generals defeated Otho's army near Cremona. On hearing the news, Otho committed suicide; he had ruled only three months.

Vitellius marched his troops into Italy, which they treated like enemy territory—looting, raping and killing. They took six months to reach the capital, where they behaved with equal ferocity, while the new Emperor indulged his appetites, especially those of the table. Hearing of all this, the legions in the East were resentful and jealous. Why should the German armies live in luxury? And if it came to making emperors, they had a candidate in their own general, an infinitely better one than the lecherous glutton now wearing the purple.

The summer before, on the news of Nero's death, Vespasian had at once suspended his campaign in Palestine. This allowed Simon to collect a large army and regain much of Idumaea, despite fierce opposition from the inhabitants and from the main body of the Zealots, led by John. Simon fought both with varying fortunes. His wife was captured, but he secured her release through savage reprisals, and in April 69 was invited into Jerusalem by a former High Priest who believed that nothing could be worse than John. Simon became master of the city, except the Temple, which John still held.

The Roman legions stayed at Caesarea watching the Jewish civil war from the sidelines. No campaign was possible while the Empire itself might be ablaze, and Vespasian claimed he was waiting for new instructions from Rome. After several months' delay he sent Titus, accompanied by Agrippa and Berenice, to salute Galba. On their way they heard of Galba's assassination—at which Titus hurried back to Syria.

Vespasian recognised Otho, and in June marched south again. In a short campaign he occupied most of the country once more, and returned to Caesarea with Jerusalem isolated, only to postpone his attack on it yet again because of a new crisis in the Empire, which required a fateful personal decision.

Although tempted to stake his own claim, he had reluctantly recognised Vitellius. But his army proclaimed him Emperor, and when he declined, giving his arguments, he had greatness thrust upon him in a rather humiliating way, as Josephus records without any sign of embarrassment: 'The officers pressed him more insistently, and the soldiers, flocking round with drawn swords, threatened him with death if he refused to live with dignity.' In the end Vespasian yielded to their demands.

Mucianus, legate of Syria, reminded him of the fate of Corbulo, another successful general in the East, and urged him to go boldly ahead. He heard that the seven legions on the Danube were for him, and he counted on Tiberius Alexander, Prefect of Egypt, with the two legions at Alexandria. He wrote to the Prefect, asking for his help, and on 1st July 69 Tiberius had legions and populace take the oath of allegiance to Vespasian.

The Danube and the Syrian legions followed suit, and Vespasian left Caesarea for Beirut, where many embassies came to him with crowns and congratulations. Mucianus reported great popular enthusiasm for him all over Syria, and there was even a promise of 40,000 mounted archers from the King of Parthia.

Agrippa and Berenice, who had gone on to Rome, found out in time how things stood, and rejoined Vespasian at Beirut. Berenice, now forty, was still a very beautiful woman, who made herself specially attractive to the Emperor, and even more so to his son. 'A 'romance' between her and Titus began to take shape.

Fortune seemed very much with Vespasian, and many omens and prophecies in his favour were brought up. Among these he suddenly remembered how Josephus had dared, even in Nero's lifetime, to address him as Emperor, and was shocked to think this Jewish prophet was still a prisoner.

Summoning Mucianus and his staff, he called for Josephus and ordered him to be liberated. 'While the officers were only thinking that such a reward for a foreigner augured brilliant honours for themselves, Titus ... said:

"Justice demands, father, that Josephus should lose his disgrace along with his fetters. If we sever his chains, it will be as though he had never been in bonds at all." For such is the practice where a man has been unjustly put in irons. When Vespasian gave his approval, an attendant came forward and severed the chains with an axe.' After two years as a prisoner, it was a big moment for Josephus, probably the biggest in his life.

Vespasian distributed governorships partly on merit, partly for services rendered or anticipated; then he left for Antioch, the capital of Syria. It was decided that Mucianus should lead the army overland to Rome.

Meanwhile the Danube legions, led by Antonius Primus, were already marching on Italy. Vitellius sent a strong force to meet them, and as with Otho earlier in the year the armies faced each other near Cremona. After an unsuccessful attempt by Vitellius's commander to go over to Vespasian, Primus seized his chance to attack, pursued Vitellius's army into Cremona, and destroyed it. This was one of the decisive battles in Roman history, for it led to a new dynasty being established.

When the news reached Rome, Sabinus, Vespasian's elder brother, seized the Capitol—the temple of Jupiter—and persuaded Vitellius to abdicate. But the German legions were out of control and refused to allow this. After fierce fighting they captured the temple, plundered and burnt it, and executed Sabinus with most of his followers. But 'Domitian, with many eminent Romans, miraculously escaped'. This is the first appearance of Vespasian's younger son, the future Emperor, in the pages of Josephus, who understandably does not mention that Domitian fled disguised as a priest of Isis.

The Vitellians' triumph did not last long. Next day,

Primus's army marched in and destroyed them, killing 50,000 in Josephus's figure, which probably includes thousands of civilians. Vitellius was dragged out of his palace and lynched. Primus's troops were kept from further slaughter by Mucianus, Vespasian's first sponsor and acknowledged deputy, who arrived with his army the following day. He brought forward Domitian and 'recommended him to the multitude as their ruler pending his father's arrival. The people, freed at length from terrors, acclaimed Vespasian emperor.'

So 69 A.D., the 'Year of the four Emperors', ended with Vespasian supreme. As with Augustus after Actium, exactly a century before, even the armies were weary of bloodshed, and everywhere people longed for peace.

After staying the autumn in Syria, Vespasian and Titus proceeded to Alexandria, where they were greeted by the good news from Rome and received congratulations from all over the Empire. Vespasian remained there several months, making sure of his position. It was widely reported that he miraculously cured a blind man and a cripple; the whole East should know that the power of the gods was on him. As to Rome, he could evidently trust Domitian and Mucianus, although Domitian issued so many new appointments that Vespasian, noted for his dry wit, remarked that it was a mercy his son didn't send a successor to *him*.

As Emperor he could not afford to spend more time on the Jewish rebellion. So in the spring of 70 he sent Titus with picked forces to complete the conquest of Judaea and carry out the attack, put off two years running, on the Jewish capital. Once the Roman civil war had finished, the days of Jerusalem must surely be numbered.

Well might Josephus recall how that peasant—Jesus, son of Ananias—released as a maniac by the procurator

The Arch of Titus in Rome.

Detail from the Arch. The spoils from Jerusalem showing the
Menorah (the seven-branched candlestick).

Jerusalem. Model of the Temple and Antonia Fortress.

Western (Wailing) Wall with the Mosque of Omar (left).

Albinus, had for seven and a half years repeated his monotonous lament, 'Woe to Jerusalem': 'He never cursed those who beat him nor blessed those who offered him food. His cries were loudest at the festivals.' Then, during the siege, 'while going his rounds and shouting in piercing tones from the wall, "Woe once more to the city and to the people and to the Temple", as he added a last word, "and woe to me also", a stone hurled from one of the Roman engines struck and killed him on the spot. So with these ominous words still upon his lips, he passed away.'

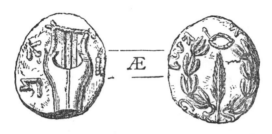

Bronze coin probably struck by Simon Ben Gioras about A.D. 69. Obverse shows 'Simon' (Shimon) in Hebrew characters around a three-stringed lyre, recalling joyful strains of thanksgiving after victories; reverse expresses same idea through palm branch enclosed in olive wreath, around which may be traced in Hebrew characters (some left to conjecture) the words Lacheruth Jerushalaim *(of the Deliverance of Jerusalem)*

E

CHAPTER 12

WOE TO JERUSALEM!

The Jews had wasted nearly a year's respite—to judge from Josephus—in battles among themselves as savage as any fought against the Romans, with no motive except their leaders' lust for power and the hatred these leaders aroused. We cannot be sure that Josephus has not kept silent on other motives, but evidently the nation regained no territory; all the struggles were for control of the Holy City.

The lay-out of Jerusalem was something like this: The old city was built on three hills, with a wall around them and deep ravines outside it, except on the north side. A second wall extended from Herod's Palace to the Antonia fortress. Beyond this lay the 'new' city, enclosed by a third wall. Of the three hills, the 'Upper City' was in the south west, separated by a deep valley from the 'Lower City' in the south and the vast fortified complex of the Temple in the east, which stood on a large plateau and covered about twenty-five acres. It was made up of a series of courts at different levels: the Outer Court, the Inner Court, and at the top the Court of the Priests, containing the great altar and behind that the sanctuary—the Holy of Holies.

There were now three factions in Jerusalem. Simon had failed to oust John from the Temple, but John was now under attack from above as well as below. A party of

Zealots, backing his rival, Eleazar, had broken away and occupied the Inner Courts and the sanctuary. With plenty of provisions they could hold out for a long time, and they allowed worship and sacrifice to go on. Even then, foreign Jews still came to the Temple from all over the world, although the worshippers were often killed or injured by missiles shot from John's engines.

When John made sallies into the main city, he set fire to buildings full of corn and stores; and when John withdrew, Simon did the same. Most of the ample corn supplies were burnt during this period, and the city was reduced to a desolate no-man's land. Flight was impossible, for 'the brigand chiefs, divided on all else, put to death as their common enemies any in favour of peace with the Romans or suspected of an intention to desert'.

The Romans arrived on the outskirts of Jerusalem just before the Jewish Passover (April 70). Titus had a large army with him: four legions, contingents from the allied kings, and five thousand picked men under Tiberius Alexander, whose troops and people in Egypt had first saluted Vespasian as Emperor. Vespasian decided that Tiberius with his long experience would make a good right-hand man for Titus.

During a first reconnaissance tour with six hundred horsemen, Titus was intercepted by a large guerilla force. Cut off with a handful of men, he saved his life only through his personal prowess and, for Josephus, divine protection— since he wore neither helmet nor cuirass (rather rashly, one would think); yet the arrows whizzed harmlessly by. The guerillas had another minor success when they nearly stormed the 10th Legion's camp on the Mount of Olives. The Romans were disconcerted by the Jews' unorthodox tactics, and again, in Josephus's account, 'if, without a syllable added in flattery or withheld in envy, the truth must be told', it was only the intrepid general who rallied his men to drive the enemy back into the ravine. He 'twice rescued the entire legion when in jeopardy'.

Quite a few syllables did get added, and Titus with his incredible brilliance, audacity, courage and charmed life, becomes a little ridiculous in the pages of Josephus's history. Josephus was an eye-witness for most of the time, having been taken along almost as a member of Titus's staff. His main function was to talk to his fellow Jews in their own language and persuade them of the advantages of surrender.

They were in no mood for surrender; but after putting aside their differences for the daring attack on the Roman camp, they resumed their civil war. John achieved one success by infiltrating some of his men into the Passover worshippers and eventually defeating Eleazar's men after violent fighting, forcing them to hide in the Temple vaults. John granted them a truce; they combined forces, and Eleazar became John's second in command. They now had about 8500 men against Simon's 15,000—and against the Romans.

Like previous attackers of Jerusalem, Titus meant to capture the northern part of the city. Although harassed by the Jews, the legions had soon levelled the ground near the first wall, after which they dug in, set the suburbs on fire, and started raising banks in preparation for the siege. In due course they were able to bring into play their battering-rams, which made an appalling noise and caused terror among the defenders.

This had the effect, however, of bringing the rival factions together, with an ease which Josephus does not really explain. They shouted across to each other that they were helping the enemy by their strife and ought to unite at least for the moment. On this 'Simon proclaimed that all were at liberty to pass from the Temple to the wall, and John, though mistrusting him, gave his permission. The parties, consigning their hatred and private quarrels to oblivion, thus became one body . . .'—and so they remained till the end.

With their forces reunited, the Jews regained confidence. They bombarded the troops working the rams, and even dashed out in an attempt to burn the Romans' engines. At first 'Jewish daring outstripped Roman discipline', but the picked troops from Alexandria held out bravely until Titus (of course!) rode up with his cavalry to charge the enemy and drive them back into the city. Soon he had three high towers built, which gave his men good protection and easy targets, so that on May 25th, the fifteenth day of the siege, the first wall was breached and the Romans controlled the whole of the New City.

When they attacked the second wall, they met desperate Jewish resistance. As Josephus admits, Simon possessed such personal magnetism that his men would have killed themselves at his command.

Josephus himself had a nasty experience at this time. One of the defenders appeared outside the wall pretending to be a deserter. Titus asked Josephus to give the man his hand as a sign mercy would be granted. Suspecting the man's genuineness, Josephus said he would rather not, and another Jew, who had deserted earlier, came forward instead. The man hurled a boulder at him for his pains; it missed but wounded a soldier behind him. Titus was furious at the whole incident.

After five days the Romans stormed the second wall, and Titus entered with a thousand legionaries, but made the tactical mistake (Josephus thinks) of not attacking the part of the city he had taken. He gave the troops orders not to kill or to burn the houses; challenged the rebels to continue the fight outside the city, which would thus be spared; and promised the people restoration of their property. The Zealots 'mistook his humanity for weakness and regarded these overtures as due to his inability to capture the rest of the town'. They attacked the Roman invaders, and with the advantage of local knowledge forced them back behind the second wall again.

Four days later the Romans retook it. Titus briefly stopped operations, hoping the Jews might surrender, and sent Josephus to use his powers of persuasion once more.

So Josephus went round the wall, trying 'to keep out of range and yet within earshot', and made his most passionate appeal yet. His arguments were much the same as Agrippa had used—their forefathers had submitted to the Romans, God was on Rome's side, the Romans would be lenient if they gave in now, merciless if they did not—but during this appeal he was jeered, cursed and shot at. So he went on to remind his countrymen how often in the past they had been delivered by the Lord without their raising a hand, and of the bondage in Babylon, 'where our people never reared their heads for liberty, until Cyrus granted it in gratitude to God'. In short, the Jews throughout their history had always triumphed without arms when they committed their cause to God. But how dare they now expect God to be their ally, when they had defiled His Temple and outraged Him by every crime under the sun?

Finally Josephus called on the 'iron-hearted men' to repent even now, for God was merciful, to fling away their weapons and have pity on their country, or at least their own children, wives and parents, soon to be victims of either famine or war: 'I have a mother, a wife, a noble family, and an ancient and illustrious house involved in these perils; and perhaps you think it is on their account my advice is offered. Kill them, take my blood as the price of your own salvation! I too am prepared to die, if my death will lead to your learning wisdom.'

'Yet though Josephus with tears thus loudly appealed to them,' he continues, 'the insurgents neither yielded nor considered it safe to alter their course ...' As with many of the speeches, his eloquence was written up afterwards, and one wonders how much of this address he actually shouted out while dodging missiles. The concern for self-preservation he shows elsewhere would have kept it short and sweet if he ventured within their range at all. The peroration has two curious points: no mention of his father, and the solitary reference to a first wife, presumably from pre-war days.

Although the Zealots proclaimed 'No Surrender', increasing famine in the city, combined with the reign of terror, made many people try to get out of Jerusalem while there was still the slightest chance. They sold their property and valuables for trifling sums, swallowing the gold to escape detection and after escape re-producing it through their bowels. Titus let most of the deserters go unmolested, and this acted as an inducement to others. But one very important desertion took place, which Josephus, surprisingly, does not mention.

Once the war had started, Hillel's school of Pharisees lost most of their influence, despite the veneration felt for their leader, Rabbi Johanan Ben Zakkai, now in his seventies. During the siege, Johanan escaped by feigning death: two of his chief disciples carried him safely through the Roman lines. After his 'resurrection' he obtained permission from

Titus to settle at Jamnia, a town on the coast where some rabbis had already gone. He established there a sort of religious college, which, at his pleading, Titus spared when Jerusalem fell. The college became a new Sanhedrin, though with far more limited powers; but its existence was essential for the survival of the Jewish faith after the Temple's destruction.

What had been happening all this while to the Jewish Christians? There is a tradition, probably mistaken, that the Jerusalem Church opted out of the national struggle and took refuge as a body in Pella, a town in Peraea. The Messiah had not returned, and some might leave the city to await his Second Coming, while others would regard the war as one of the trials to be expected before that Great Day. Others again may have reverted in disappointment to the old faith and fought against the Romans. Yet most Nazarenes must surely have dissociated themselves from the civil war, disgusted by the atrocities committed by Jew against Jew. For in preventing desertion and getting rid of their enemies, the Zealots showed no mercy.

With famine and slaughter inside the city, the alternative became equally grim. When foraging parties venturing into the ravines were caught, Titus had them whipped, tortured and crucified. Others were sent back with their hands cut off—to urge surrender even now, so that Jerusalem and the Temple might be saved.

The rebel leaders responded by heaping abuse on Titus and Vespasian from the ramparts, 'crying out that they scorned death, which they honourably preferred to slavery; that they would do the Romans every injury they could while they had breath in their bodies; that men so soon to perish were unconcerned for their native place'. But the Temple 'would yet be saved by Him who dwelt therein, and while they had Him for their ally, they would laugh at all threats unsupported by action; for the issue rested with God'.

It was honest of Josephus to record these brave words from his bitter enemies; as often, we get a sense of his unwilling admiration. We see again, too, how the rebels were sustained even now by hope of supernatural aid.

Sometimes they seemed to have it, or at any rate be inspired to amazing feats. In one action the Romans had to retreat to their camp with the Jews in pursuit. They eventually drove the Jews back into the city, but Roman morale was at a low ebb. There was a growing belief that they would never take the city, and although Josephus understandably does not mention it, we hear from another source that some Roman soldiers even deserted to the Jews. It was a bad time for Josephus, whom the Romans blamed for every defeat, suspecting that he had passed information to the enemy. They kept calling for him to be punished as their betrayer, but Titus refused to give in to these demands.

After a council of war, the general decided to build a wall around the whole city with thirteen huge towers, a terrific task which the legions completed, however, in three days. Conditions inside the city became abruptly worse, and the Romans were once more in the highest spirits. Many went up to the ramparts and displayed all their food, to torment the starving Jews. The rebel leaders still maintained an iron control, and Simon put to death the former High Priest, who had invited him into the city as an enemy of John. The Secretary of the Sanhedrin and sixteen other notables were also condemned, Josephus's parents were imprisoned, a proclamation was issued that nobody should congregate in one spot, and people seen mourning their dead were summarily executed.

Josephus continued his appeals; on one occasion a stone hit him on the head. He fell unconscious, and the rebels made a rush for him. Titus sent out a rescue party, which got him safely away, but the rebels were elated, while the people (he says) were despondent. He soon recovered, however, and came forward threatening quick vengeance. Despite all precautions by John and Simon there was another wave of desertions.

Meanwhile the Romans had built more earthworks, leaving desolation in the suburbs, once so beautiful, with all the trees felled and the gardens destroyed. Part of the army now attacked the Antonia fortress, which John's men were defending, captured it, and pressed on to the Temple, only to be driven back to the Antonia after a furious battle lasting all night. Titus had most of the fortress rased. It was now the beginning of August, and he seemed in sight of victory at last.

When he heard that the Jews had given up their daily sacrifices for lack of officiates—a great symbolic disaster to them—he sent Josephus once again to call for surrender, with a promise that the Temple would be spared. John fiercely rejected any terms, but at this point many of the surviving aristocrats found it easier to escape. Titus received them kindly, and sent them to a small town twelve miles away. The rebels made out that the Romans had killed these refugees, so he brought them back and had them go round the ramparts with Josephus, begging the rebels at least to withdraw from the Temple. Titus would naturally have preferred to avoid a whole new operation, but as neither threats nor pleading produced any result, he could only go ahead with plans to capture it.

A surprise attack failed, the business of building earthworks started again, and now the troops had to collect timber from several miles away, while continually harassed by the defenders. Battering-rams and siege engines failed to breach the massive Temple walls; parties with scaling ladders were repulsed with casualties. The Romans burnt the gates between the Outer and Inner Court, and the fire smouldered away in the Inner Court; they were given orders to put it out.

Meanwhile Titus held a council of war. Some of his staff were for destroying the Temple anyhow, others only if the Jews stayed and defended it. According to Josephus, Titus declared that he would not burn down such a magnificent building in any circumstances, for if it stood, it would be 'an ornament to the Empire'. Another tradition has it that he insisted the Temple should be destroyed, believing that its existence sustained both Jews and Christians. Josephus may 'protest too much' over Titus's anxiety to spare the great shrine; he was bound to defend his patron against what Jews everywhere would see as the unforgivable crime. Yet there was sense in Titus's argument, and perhaps, too, his darling Berenice pleaded with him. We can give him the benefit of the doubt, and say that what happened was not what he intended.

Throughout the next day August 29th, there were Roman attacks and desperate Jewish counter-attacks, until the Jews were at last shut up in the Inner Court. Titus withdrew to the Antonia, intending a full-scale assault at dawn. Soon afterwards the Jews attacked the troops who were putting out the fire in the Inner Court; but they were routed and pursued right back to the Sanctuary. At this juncture a Roman soldier snatched up a firebrand, got on one of his comrades' shoulders, and flung it through a low golden door which gave access to the rooms round the Sanctuary. A great flame shot up, and loud cries arose from the Jews, 'who flocked to the rescue, lost to all thought of self-preservation'.

Someone rushed into Titus's tent to inform him, and he dashed off to the Temple, followed by all his staff and a mass of excited legionaries. He shouted and gesticulated that the fire must be put out, but in the uproar and confusion they took no notice: 'Crushed together about the entrances, many Roman soldiers were trampled down by their companions; many, stumbling on the still smouldering ruins of the porticoes, suffered the fate of the vanquished. As they drew near to the Sanctuary, they ... shouted to those in front of them to throw in the firebrands ... On all sides was slaughter and flight. Most of the slain were civilians ... Around the altar a pile of corpses was accumulating; down the steps of the Sanctuary flowed a stream of blood.'

With the frenzied troops completely out of control, Titus and his generals entered the Holy of Holies and saw all it contained, 'things far exceeding the reports current among foreigners'—Josephus speaks here as a proud Jew—'and not inferior to their exalted reputation among ourselves'.

The flames had not yet reached the sanctuary itself, and Titus rushed out, making urgent personal appeals to stop the fire, while a centurion threatened to club the disobedient. It was no good; the soldiers' hatred and hopes of plunder carried the day. Then somebody 'thrust a firebrand into the hinges of the gate. At once a flame shot up from the interior, Caesar and his generals withdrew, and there was no one left to prevent those outside from kindling a blaze. Thus, against Caesar's wishes, was the temple set on fire.'

Eye-witness of the tragedy, Josephus in his history mourns

'the most marvellous edifice we have ever seen or heard of', but admires the exactness of Destiny's cycle, since Solomon's Temple, he says, was burnt by Nebuchadnezzar on the same day of the same month. From its rebuilding after the Captivity, the Second Temple lasted 639 years. Part of (Herod's) western wall survived, to become the Wailing Wall where future generations of Jews mourned the Temple's destruction. It was to this they rushed and prayed in June 1967 when Jerusalem was at last theirs again.

'While the Temple blazed, the victors plundered everything that fell in their way, and slaughtered wholesale all who were caught.' The din of roaring flames, war-cries, howls and screams was terrifying. A large body of Zealots managed to force their way into the Outer Court and from there to the Lower City. The Romans set fire to all the buildings round the temple, including the treasury chambers, 'in which lay vast sums of money, vast piles of raiment and other valuables; for this was the general repository of Jewish wealth, to which the rich had consigned the contents of their dismantled houses'. The Romans burnt all the colonnades of the Outer Court. A crowd of about 6000 had taken refuge on the colonnade which was last to go. When the Romans set fire to this from below, not one of the crowd survived.

They had gone there, Josephus says, because a false prophet had told them of God's command 'to go up to the Temple court, to receive there the signs of their deliverance'. He then talks of all the prophets 'suborned by the tyrants to delude the people, by bidding them await help from God', and of the many portents which heralded the disaster. Among these were some that have a biblical ring: a star like a sword standing over the city, a light shining round the altar in the night, a massive gate of the Inner

137

Court opening of its own accord (Tacitus also mentions this 'happening'), chariots in the sky; and one portent that might have strained even Josephus's credulity—a sacrificial cow giving birth to a lamb!

Then there was Jesus, son of Ananias, with his cries of 'Woe to Jerusalem!' But if that was calculated to increase alarm and despondency, Josephus claims that the Jews were specially encouraged by 'an ambiguous oracle, also found in their sacred scriptures, to the effect that at that time one from their country would become ruler of the world'. This oracle is also referred to by Tacitus, and of course, says Josephus, the Jews thought it was one of their race, not realising it meant Vespasian, proclaimed Emperor on Jewish soil. Perhaps a reference here to Christianity?

The Romans, now masters of the whole Temple area, carried their standards into the Inner Court, set them up opposite the eastern gate, sacrificed to them there, and hailed their great general. Titus himself had been in the Holy of Holies: to Jews it meant that God had surely deserted the place; to Romans that the last stronghold of barbarian fanaticism had been conquered. A remnant of the priests, holding out on the sanctuary wall, gave in from starvation after five days, were taken by guards to Titus, and implored him to spare their lives. The time for pardon was past, he told them, and priests should perish with their Temple. They were led off to execution.

The Zealot chiefs were on the other side of a bridge connecting the Upper City with the Temple. They could not escape into the country because of the Roman wall, but they boldly invited Titus to a parley. He accepted, and after a victor's contemptuous speech promised to spare their lives if they surrendered. John and Simon answered that they had sworn never to accept a pledge from him, but 'asked permission to pass through his line of walls with their wives and children, undertaking to retire to the desert and to leave the city to him'.

It was an extraordinary request, but based on age-old Jewish traditions. Patriotism and religious fervour were once again merged, as in the glorious days of the Maccabees, who had rallied the people for new resistance in the Judaean countryside. If God in His wrath had deserted the Holy City and even allowed His Temple to be destroyed, Israel could still survive as a community of the Covenant by flight into the wilderness. But the Romans could not possibly have allowed bases in the country for guerilla warfare to continue. Titus indignantly refused, proclaiming that the Jews should neither desert nor hope for terms, since he would spare none. He then gave his troops permission to burn and sack the city.

The rebels must have been still in very considerable force, for after beating off the Romans they seized Herod's palace and killed over 8000 people who had collected there. They prepared to hold out in the Upper City, used underground passages as operational bases, and forced Titus to start building earthworks again. Josephus continued to make vain entreaties to 'the tyrants' for what remained of the city. The Idumaean leaders were thwarted in an attempt to negotiate surrender, and five would-be negotiators were put to death. Masses still succeeded in deserting, however, and despite his proclamation Titus let over forty thousand (Josephus's figures again!) go free.

It took another eighteen days for the Romans to complete the new earthworks and bring up their siege engines. Soon part of the wall round the Upper City was breached. The rebels lost heart, and either went underground or tried vainly to cut through the Roman lines. According to Josephus, the three mighty towers they abandoned would have been quite impregnable: he attributes the tyrants' panic to 'God's power over unholy men' and the Romans' good fortune. On the same day, September 25th, the Romans planted their standards on the towers and raised a paean of triumph, amazed at the ease with which they had won this last part of their victory.

Pouring into the alleys, they indulged for the rest of the day in a new orgy of burning, looting and slaughter. No mercy was shown to the living, but they retired empty-handed and in horror from houses filled with the corpses of famine victims. By nightfall, when the orgy stopped, fire had gained the mastery. Dawn broke on a city in flames.

Titus gave orders to stop the killing, except of people who resisted or were found armed. But the troops took matters into their own hands, and killed the old and infirm as well. Titus put Fronto, a freedman, in charge of the enormous mass of prisoners, who were herded into one of the Temple's ruined courts. Eleven thousand died of starvation, some refusing to eat when food was offered them. Fronto put to death all leading rebels, who now informed against each other. He then picked out seven hundred of the tallest and most handsome young men for Titus's triumph; sent all the rest of the youth over seventeen to the mines in Egypt; and sold the younger children as slaves. Titus presented thousands to the provinces of the Empire, where they would later be 'butchered to make a Roman holiday'.

Josephus's own feelings can be imagined, as from the enemy side he watched his native city in flames, his former fellow-citizens lying in agony. Still in high favour with the general, if still suspect to many of the Roman officers, he did what little he could as a Jew who had made his peace with Caesar.

'Titus repeatedly urged me,' he tells us in the *Life*, 'to take whatever I wanted from the wreck of my country, and I, now that my native place had fallen, having nothing more precious to take and preserve as a consolation for my personal misfortunes, asked Titus for the freedom of some of my countrymen; I also received by his gracious favour a gift of sacred books. Not long after, I petitioned for my brother and fifty friends, and my request was granted.' (He does not say what happened to his first wife or parents.) Later, among the thousands imprisoned in the Temple court, he obtained the release of another 190 friends and acquaintances he recognised.

Then he saw three people he knew being crucified; and 'cut to the heart', went in tears to Titus. Titus at once ordered that they should be taken down and given the best medical treatment. Two died in the doctor's hands, the third survived. In a fascinating recent book, *The Passover Plot*, Hugh Schonfield finds a parallel with the Crucifixion of Jesus and the two 'thieves', and a basis for his speculation that when taken off the Cross Jesus was not yet dead.

Curiously enough, there is a parallel in the Resurrection story with the eventual capture of Simon. He and a party tunnelled their way down into secret passages a week or two later, when their food was nearly exhausted, 'Simon, imagining that he could cheat the Romans by creating a scare, dressed himself in a white tunic, and buckling over a purple mantle, arose out of the ground at the very spot where the temple formerly stood. The spectators were at first aghast and remained motionless; but afterwards they came nearer and asked who he was. This Simon declined to tell them, but bade them summon the general . . .'

He was recognised and reserved for execution at the victory celebrations. John, who had surrendered earlier—he hid in the caves till on the point of starvation—was condemned to life imprisonment. Josephus gives the number of prisoners taken throughout the war as 97,000, and of those who died in the siege as 1,100,000. The majority of this immense number, he explains, were foreign Jews who had poured into Jerusalem for the Passover Festival. Even allowing for that, it seems one of his wilder figures.

Titus left the three great towers as a memorial to his good fortune; one of them, now called David's Tower, is still standing today, near the Jaffa Gate. He had the city's suburbs burnt and the rest of the wall round the city so completely flattened that future visitors to the site would have had no reason to believe it had ever been inhabited.

And so Jerusalem, established as the Jewish capital by David who had expelled its Canaanite population, captured five times, sacked once before (by the Babylonians), was now destroyed for the second time, 1179 years after David, 2177 after its first Canaanite foundation. With this brief historical summary, Josephus concludes the last but one book of *The Jewish War*: 'Yet neither its antiquity, nor its great wealth, nor its people spread over the whole habitable world, nor yet the glory of its religious rites, could help at all to avert its ruin. Thus ended the siege of Jerusalem.'

Coin of Titus

CHAPTER 13

ROMAN TRIUMPH, JEWS' LAST STAND

Vespasian had spent the spring in Alexandria. His power in Rome seemed firm, and his generals quickly mastered other nationalist movements, on the Danube, in Germany and Gaul. In June he made a leisurely progress by way of Rhodes, Ionia and Greece, to receive a rapturous welcome on arrival in Italy. In October he reached Rome, to a climax of jubilation, especially as the news had now come in from Palestine.

Leaving the 10th legion as garrison in Jerusalem, Titus returned to Caesarea. Here and at other cities he gave spectacular shows in the arenas, where thousands of Jewish prisoners had to fight each other as gladiators or else were pitted against wild beasts. Despite all the ways the victims perished, Josephus comments, it seemed to the Romans too light a punishment.

But Titus resisted demands by the Greek inhabitants of Antioch to expel all Jews from the city. He pointed out that there was nowhere for them to go, since their own country had been destroyed, and he refused to remove the brass tablets in the chief synagogue recording the traditional privileges of Antioch's Jews.

On his way back to Egypt he paid a farewell visit to

Jerusalem, and Josephus has him sadly deploring its destruction: 'Not boasting ... of having carried so glorious and great a city by storm, but heaping curses on the criminal authors of the revolt, who had brought this chastisement upon it.'

From Egypt he sailed for Rome, where he was met by Vespasian in person amidst further scenes of wild enthusiasm. The Senate had decreed a separate triumphal procession for each, but they agreed on a joint celebration, which took place in June 71.

Josephus owned property at Jerusalem. Since a Roman garrison was to be quartered there, Titus compensated him with a gift of land on the coastal plain; Vespasian later gave him another grant of land in Palestine, tax-free. He travelled to Rome in Titus's suite, was shown all respect, and on arrival received equally preferential treatment from Vespasian. He was given a pension and part of a house where Vespasian had lived, and was also made a Roman citizen. Joseph Ben Matthias now adopted the name of Flavius Josephus, by which he is known to history—Flavius after Vespasian's second name. When we feel sickened by his effusive propaganda on behalf of Vespasian and his sons, we should remember that he had very good reason for being exceptionally grateful to them.

Still, the first great spectacle which the new Roman citizen saw must have been painful indeed for this Jewish aristocrat, of priestly family, descendant of the kings who had restored Jewish freedom. Josephus gives no hint, however, of bitterness or distress when writing up the triumph of his two imperial patrons. Yet the most striking things in that magnificent procession—with all its tapestries, works of art, dressed-up animals, images of the gods—were the huge 'floats' with tableaux showing highly realistic scenes of destruction and desolation from the Jewish war.

Most of the spoils were heaped together in a jumbled mass, but the Temple trophies stood out: golden altar, seven-branched gold 'candlestick', silver trumpets, purple 'veils' or curtains of the Sanctuary, and—last of all—a Scroll of the Law. Then came a large party carrying ivory and gold images of Victory, followed by Vespasian and Titus in their triumphal chariots, and Domitian riding a magnificent horse.

Even the prisoners led in the procession had been put into fine clothing to conceal their wounds from view. One of them was Simon. Now he was whipped, dragged to the forum with a rope round his neck and executed. By ancient custom everyone waited at the Temple of Jupiter to hear the enemy general's death proclaimed; the people cheered jubilantly. Then, after prayers and sacrifices, the Emperor and his sons withdrew to the palace, and the official part of the triumph was over. But the people of Rome went on celebrating all day—not only the crushing of the Jewish rebellion, but the restoration of civil peace after the whole Empire had nearly broken up.

Vespasian decided to build a Temple of Peace commemorating the triumph. Completed in 75, it housed masterpieces of painting and sculpture, and also the Treasures of the Jewish Temple, except for the Scroll of the Law and the curtains, which the Emperor kept in his palace. These and all the other treasures have disappeared, but we can still see what they looked like. A bas-relief from the Arch of Titus, erected by the Senate after his death, shows them being borne along by his victorious legionaries.

Another Jew who probably witnessed the triumph was John Mark. It is now generally thought that he wrote his Gospel for the Christian community in Rome soon afterwards (in 71 or 72), when his readers would have fresh in their minds, for instance, the veil of the Temple, 'rent in twain' after the Crucifixion. Mark also makes Jesus prophesy the Temple's destruction, and one of the vivid tableaux may have shown the legions hailing Titus in the Inner Court. Mark recalls it in the words of Jesus, apparently prophetic: 'When you see the abomination of desolation standing where he ought not ... then let them that are in Judaea flee into the mountains.' Titus was 'the Abomination of Desolation', a heathen who had even entered the Holy of Holies.

Another point in Mark's Gospel which may have had a special meaning for its first readers is that in it Jesus seems to deny descent from David. Perhaps this was because Vespasian is supposed to have hunted out and put to death all those he could find of David's line. This action would be directed especially against Christians.

Josephus, now starting his history, hoped to protect Jews all over the world from the 'antisemitism' rampant after four years of war; so he stressed the Zealots' crimes and the brutality of the last procurators. In rather the same way, Mark wanted to shift the blame for the Crucifixion on to the Jewish leaders—but not the Zealots. It would have been disastrous to probe too deeply into Christian connections with the Zealots, and he calls the apostle Simon 'the Cananaean', without explaining that the Aramaic word Qana meant Zealot. Luke, writing much later, could call him 'Simon the Zealot', but in none of the Gospel accounts does Jesus have any dealings with the Zealots as a body.

Mark also started the process of whitewashing Pilate. Again, according to *his* account, it was a Roman centurion who first recognised the crucified Jesus as Son of God. Rome's Christians could see that Jesus, although born a Jew, had no essential connection with his race's fanatical excesses: he was a prophet without honour in his own country.

Mark had travelled with Paul and may have been with him at the end, when his reputation was in eclipse and most Christians accepted the Jerusalem Church's authority. After 70 the chief centre of Christianity in Palestine was probably Caesarea, where Paul had been well known. The Nazarenes survived, with Simeon as elder, but could not easily communicate with Christians in other countries or maintain their version of what Christianity meant. Mark realised how well Paul's version fitted the new situation for largely Gentile communities, and how it explained what Professor Brandon calls 'the embarrassing involvement of the incarnated Son of God with the Roman procurator Pontius Pilate'.

Unlike Paul in his Epistles, Mark felt the need to record in detail the life, teachings and above all—death of the historical Jesus, based on what he could remember from contact with the apostles, on all the oral traditions, and perhaps on written accounts as well. He interpreted them for his own community's needs: to show that Jesus was not implicated with the rebels against Rome, and that Jewish stubbornness had caused a change in God's intentions towards the world. The end of the Temple and of Temple worship confirmed that observance of the Jewish Law was no longer necessary for salvation, that the true Christian hope was in a temple 'not made with hands'.

Writing a Gospel was a new departure of tremendous importance, for copies would soon be made and circulated outside the Roman community. Mark thus played a vital part in reviving and transforming the Christian faith so that it lived on after the disaster of 70. The Church of Jerusalem, in Brandon's summing up, strove to contain the new wine

147

of Christianity within the old wine-skin of Israel's ethnic faith: 'But in the overthrow of the Jewish state the old wine-skins of Judaism were burst asunder and perished, liberating the new wine to flow freely abroad and to reach maturity in places more congenial to the original genius of its creator.'

But the transformed Christianity still kept one essential feature from its Nazarene origins: the faithful in Judaea were bidden to flee to the mountains, ignore the false prophets who would arise, and wait vigilantly for the Second Coming, for 'you know not when the time is'. The time might be soon, heralded by all the present trials; and some of the faithful, perhaps Nazarenes as well as other patriotic Jews, *had* fled to the mountains. The fall of Jerusalem did not mean the end of the war, for three of the fortresses Herod had built were still in rebel hands: Herodium near Bethlehem, Machaerus, and Masada.

Lucilius Bassus, the new commander in Judaea, soon occupied Herodium; Machaerus, perched on a cliff, with its massive fortifications and the vast stock of arms laid up by Herod, gave him more trouble. By a stroke of luck a rebel leader was captured, and the garrison agreed to surrender if his life was spared and they could leave the fortress unmolested. Bassus granted the terms, and quickly rounded up three thousand rebels who had escaped from Jerusalem or Masada.

His next task was to carry out instructions for Judaea as a whole, now a province under a Senatorial procurator. The whole country was to be farmed out, and the proceeds sent to the Emperor. Vespasian turned to good account the vast wealth which had flowed into the Temple for so long: Jews everywhere had to send their annual two drachmas to the Temple of Jupiter at Rome—Josephus was no doubt exempt because of his special status. Besides adding to the imperial revenue, the exaction of this extra tax would discourage converts to Judaism, which was still permitted as a religion. As a further humiliation Jews had to use coinage bearing the legend of 'captured Judaea', with effigies of a bound captive maiden and the triumphant Emperor leaning his spear on her.

The legend was not fully justified for many months yet, while an army of Zealots remained at Masada, the fortress on the south west of the Dead Sea. The man who had taken command here was Eleazar, son of Ya'ir, a cousin of Menahem (son of Judas of Galilee); his relationship to the Zealots' founder gave him unquestioned authority. Under Simon, the Zealots at Masada had extended their power to the north, including Qumran. The community there, wiped out in 68, stored its sacred books at Masada, and conceivably the Nazarenes did the same. Some of them may have thought that Jesus would return to Masada, since the Last Days seemed very near at hand. The excavations of the 1960's have shown Masada's defenders as a society with strong religious convictions.

The great flat rock at the top of a sheer hill, 1300 feet above the Dead Sea, had been developed by Herod into a splendid palace complex as well as a fortress. He honeycombed it with dark chambers for water storage, and built aqueducts to them from a nearby *wadi* (valley). From these chambers, cut out by the hands of his slaves, other slaves would toil to the summit carrying water, on their backs or on donkeys. Of the only two paths, one was a zigzagging trail called 'the snake'. Besides arms, the Zealots found vast stores of food and wine preserved in the cool stone chambers from Herod's day, and the top of the rock was fertile soil, so that they could grow vegetables there. They divided up the rooms of the palace and garrison buildings, and put up a synagogue and ritual baths. In 72 just under a thousand men, women and children were still living a communal life there, rather like a modern *kibbutz*. It was the only open place in the 'Judaean desert' which offered permanent shelter from the winds and shade from the sun.

Bassus had died, and that year the new Roman general, Flavius Silva, marched against Masada with the tenth legion. The stone markings of his camp, and his wall round the fortress can still be seen; so can a huge hog-backed ramp he built on a rocky ledge four hundred and fifty feet below the battlements. On the ramp the Romans erected heavy siege engines, with a tower for their light 'artillery'.

Eleazar's men were driven from the battlements, while the rams thudded away at the Jewish wall till it was breached. The defenders had hurriedly thrown up another wall inside, made mainly of wood to absorb the rams' blows. But when Silva's troops hurled flaming torches at it, they quickly set it ablaze. At first a north wind blew the fire straight down on the Romans, threatening to destroy their engines. But then, 'as if by divine providence' (says Josephus), the wind went right round to the south, carrying the flames back on to the wall, which was soon charred rubble. The Romans 'returned rejoicing to their camp. Resolved to attack the enemy next day, they set their watch more carefully than usual that night, lest any of the besieged should escape.'

But Eleazar Ben Ya'ir had no thought of escape. He called together the bravest of his comrades and addressed them with a proposal for mass suicide: 'We have long been determined neither to serve the Romans nor any other save God, for He alone is man's true and righteous Lord ... Let our wives die before they are ravished, and our children before they have tasted slavery, and after we have slain them, let us bestow that glorious boon upon each other and preserve our liberty as a noble end to our lives. But first let us destroy our goods and the fortress by fire; for the Romans will be grieved to lose at once our persons and our wealth. Our provisions only let us spare; for they will testify that it was not starvation which subdued us, but that we preferred death to slavery.'

Some responded eagerly, but others could not bring themselves to kill their own families as well as themselves. Afraid that the rest too might weaken, Eleazar made an even more passionate speech, including a reminder of their belief in the soul's immortality and of the harrowing prospects if they did not do as he said: 'Unenslaved by the foe let us die; as free men with our wives and children, let us quit this life together.'

At this point, Josephus tells us, he was cut short by his comrades, who 'were all in haste to do the deed'. Nor did their ardour cool: 'While they caressed and embraced their wives and took their children in their arms, clinging in tears to those parting kisses, at that same instant, as though served by hands other than their own, they carried out their purpose ... Not one was found a truant ... all carried through their task with their dearest ones. Wretched victims of necessity, to whom to kill with their own hands their wives and children seemed the lightest of evils . . . They quickly piled together all the stores and set them on fire; then, having chosen by lot ten of their number to dispatch the rest, they laid themselves down each beside his prostrate wife and children, and, flinging their arms around them, offered their throats in readiness.'

When the ten had done their duty, they drew lots again to see which of them should kill the other nine and finally himself. Josephus shows no sign of remembering the way his own suicide pact in the cave worked, as he writes: 'So great was the mutual confidence they all had that neither in acting nor in suffering would one differ from another.' The last survivor, after making sure there was no one left 'who needed his hand', set the palace ablaze, then 'drove his sword clean through his body and fell beside his family'.

They died believing the Romans would find nobody from their whole community alive. But in fact two women and five children had escaped by hiding in one of the underground cisterns. The next morning, perhaps May 2nd 73, the Romans charged through a fire-blackened gap in the wall, still visible today. Baffled by the silence, the absence of opposition, and the flames inside, they shouted—and the two women came out. One of them 'lucidly reported both the speech and how the deed was done'. The Romans were incredulous, but when they fought their way through the flames to enter the palace and saw the mass of bodies, 'instead of exulting as over enemies, they admired the nobility of their resolve and the contempt of death displayed by so many'.

All organised resistance in Judaea was now at an end. Silva returned with his army to Caesarea, leaving a garrison at Masada. Long afterwards, when the Empire had fallen to barbarians, Byzantine monks built a small church there; they lived in caves among the ruins, then disappeared. Bedouins camped there, and in the nineteenth century a few travellers and archaeologists climbed to the rock. Then the state of Israel came into being, its citizens made pilgrimages to the summit, and recruits to its armed forces took a new pledge: 'Masada shall not fall again.'

Yigael Yadin's magnificent archaeological expedition

found charred sandals, pottery, scraps of food, sacred scrolls, silver coins minted by the defenders, bits of cloth, rings, cosmetic jars, blackened fireplaces; twenty five skeletons in a cave; and in the ruins of the palace, a leader's armour, perhaps Eleazar's. We may well wonder how the woman who told the story of the mass suicide could have witnessed the scene and listened to Eleazar's speeches; she and her companion must have been very quick or clever to escape with the children to their hiding-place. But whatever doubts there may be about that, the gist of Josephus's account was confirmed by the most poignant relic of Masada's fall, which Yadin's volunteers discovered near the main gates: eleven small pieces of pottery, each bearing a different name— the lots drawn by the last ten to survive. The name on the eleventh is Ben Ya'ir.

Through the long centuries of persecution, Jews have more often suffered patiently and with the courage of despair than died fighting in equal desperation. Until Israel's birth-pangs, perhaps only the Jewish rising against the Nazis in the Warsaw ghetto in 1943 is comparable to Masada. But for the Israelis the very name has an emotional power such as Thermopylae had for the ancient Greeks—the mountain pass where two hundred Spartans, dying in obedience to orders, held up the Persian army; or such as Dunkirk for the British: a defeat more honoured than any victory.

So the 'Jewish War' ended—after seven years. But before he closed his history of it, Josephus had two minor outbreaks in Africa to record as an aftermath. Quite a number of the Zealots managed to get away from Judaea to Alexandria, where they engaged in anti-Roman activities. The leaders of the Jewish council of elders summoned a general assembly and persuaded a majority that these men were a menace to their own peace and security. The people rushed out to seize the revolutionaries, who were soon captured.

Josephus again pays tribute to their unflinching endurance of the tortures to which they were submitted in order to make them acknowledge the Emperor's sovereignty. None did so; they met the ordeal 'with bodies that seemed insensible of pain and souls that almost rejoiced in it. But most of all the spectators were struck by the children of tender age, not one of whom could be prevailed upon to call Caesar lord. So far did the strength of courage rise superior to the weakness of their frames.'

The governor of Alexandria reported the disturbances to Vespasian. The Emperor, Josephus writes, 'suspicious of the interminable tendency of the Jews to revolution, and fearing that they might again collect in force and draw others away with them', ordered an ancient Jewish temple to be demolished. He could not tolerate subversion outside Judaea, especially in such an important country as Egypt, where the Jews were still a very large minority of the population.

Josephus is almost completely silent about what these Jewish communities of the Dispersion did or suffered during the war. His silence is suspect: it would be dangerous to revive ugly memories. Like Jews in Britain at the end of the Palestine Mandate in the late 1940's, when their fellow Jews were fighting the British, these Jews in the Roman Empire had sharply divided loyalties and were exposed to local 'antisemitism'. They still sent their annual contribution to the Temple, which would be called 'aiding the enemy'. When this was transformed into a tax all Jews had to pay to a pagan god's temple, how the Greeks gloated, how hurt was Jewish pride!

But they ran a terrible risk if they actively encouraged their compatriots in Judaea, and Josephus would probably have reported any major risings. No doubt they watched despairingly and were extremely glad to see the end of the war, hoping that their fellow citizens' hostility would gradually die down.

The fall of Masada renewed their troubles, for one of those who had escaped, a man called Jonathan, gained a following in Cyrene (Libya), especially among the poor, 'and led them out into the desert, promising them a display of signs and apparitions'. A force sent by Catullus, the governor, overpowered the unarmed crowd. When captured, Jonathan gave information, probably false, implicating Cyrene's wealthier Jews. Catullus promptly put three thousand of them to death, exaggerating the affair, 'so that he too might be thought to have won a Jewish war'.

Catullus took Jonathan and other prisoners to Rome, where they now informed against 'the most reputable Jews both in Alexandria and Rome'—including Josephus, who—Jonathan said—had given him arms and money. Vespasian investigated the charges, and only acquitted the defendants after Titus had spoken in their defence. Jonathan was burnt alive.

It is hard to imagine Josephus, usually well aware which side his bread was buttered, taking part in any such plot, but it shows the precariousness of his position at Rome. After describing the episode in the *Life*, he talks of the many other accusations levelled at him by people who envied his good fortune; 'but by the providence of God, I came safe through all'.

Catullus received only a reprimand, but soon afterwards was attacked by an incurable disease. In his delirium he saw the ghosts of his murdered victims standing at his side, and would leap out of bed in agony. And so he died miserably, a striking demonstration of 'how God in his providence inflicts punishment on the wicked'.

This sentence is followed by the last paragraph of *The Jewish War*: 'Here we close the history, which we promised to relate with perfect accuracy for the information of those who wish to learn how this war was waged by the Romans against the Jews. Of its style my readers must be left to judge; but, as far as truth goes, I would not hesitate boldly to assert that, throughout the narrative, this has been my single aim.'

A bold assertion indeed—especially remembering his exaggerations over numbers. But readers then, as today, might give him credit for trying hard most of the time.

Potsherd inscribed BEN YA'IR

CHAPTER 14

FLAVIAN TIMES

Some time during Vespasian's reign, Josephus divorced his third wife, 'being displeased at her behaviour'. She had borne him three children, but only one, called Hyrcanus, survived. 'Afterwards,' says a brief paragraph in the *Life*, 'I married a woman of Jewish extraction who had settled in Crete. She came of very distinguished parents, indeed the most notable people in that country. In character she surpassed many of her sex, as her subsequent life showed. By her I had two sons, Justus the elder, and then Simonides, surnamed Agrippa. Such is my domestic history.'

When Vespasian died, Titus continued to honour the historian, and rejected continuing accusations against him. 'Domitian succeeded Titus and added to my honours,' writes Josephus. 'He punished my Jewish accusers, and for a similar offence gave orders for the chastisement of a slave, a eunuch and my son's tutor. He also exempted my property in Judaea from taxation—a mark of the highest honour to a privileged individual. Moreover, Domitia, Caesar's wife, never ceased conferring favours upon me.'

According to Tertullian, the Christian theologian writing around 200 A.D., Josephus was by far the most famous Jew of his time. Statues of him were erected in Rome, his books were placed in the state library. Yet there is no mention of him in any of the extant works of his con-

F

temporaries—and even the date of his death is uncertain. So the two paragraphs from the *Life* and a few remarks scattered through his three later works give us our only information about his years spent as a man of letters in Rome.

The Jewish War was originally written in Aramaic, partly to warn Jews outside the Empire from trying any tricks in league with the Parthians. An important motive for a Greek version was to defend Jews in the Empire against their neighbours' 'antisemitism', by showing that the rebel Jews had also been rebelling against the true Jewish traditions and against God. Vespasian had refused to deprive the Jews in Antioch and Alexandria of their traditional privileges, a policy Josephus finds astonishingly generous after all the trouble the Jews had given to the Romans. It was up to him to put the case for his people in the Empire's most commonly spoken language, Greek.

He was not a Greek scholar when he came to Rome after the war, and it was a formidable task to produce such a long history in a foreign tongue. He worked hard at both language and literature, but had to rely a good deal on 'ghost writers'. With their help he drew for style and pattern on classical masters like Thucydides and Sophocles. The result, apart from its merits as history, was a fine literary achievement.

He had encouragement and help from Vespasian and Titus, who let him read their war diaries, and also the state archives. He could consult Roman generals, and above all was in close touch with Agrippa, who wrote sixty-two letters about the book to 'dearest Josephus', 'testifying to the truth of the record'. With many other Jewish informants and his personal experience on both sides, Josephus could well claim unique qualifications. He is one of a fairly small company, stretching from Thucydides to Churchill, who played a leading part in a war and afterwards wrote a history of it which became a 'classic'.

He probably completed the first Greek edition in 75, submitted copies to his patrons (who thoroughly approved), and sold it to a good many of his fellow Jews—there would be slave scribes to produce the copies. As propaganda for Rome's strength, the history merited another edition, for even then there were parts of the Empire whose loyalty was suspect: they should see what happened to those who pitted their power against Rome. It was a lesson which all the subject peoples could learn the more readily because Vespasian's government did bring a real return of imperial peace and prosperity.

In contrast to Augustus, who had to work out a new system of government, Vespasian was the patient skilled mechanic repairing a serious break-down in its machinery. Confidence was restored among citizens and soldiers alike, the armies were recalled to discipline, and by making Titus Prefect of the Praetorian Guard, the Emperor secured firm control over that power-house. Augustus and Claudius were his chief models in administration, and his coins promised the Eternity of the Roman People.

Vespasian was reputed to be miserly, and he certainly increased taxation so as to stabilise the financial system. He also abruptly ended the extravagance of his predecessors at court. But he laid out vast sums to help devastated areas, was a great builder of roads and bridges, and started building the huge Flavian Amphitheatre, the Colosseum, completed the year after his death—its ruins still make a striking spectacle today. He was a patron of education and the arts, extended Roman culture and privileges outside Italy, and encouraged a vigorous municipal life in the provinces. The old aristocracy was dying out, and new men attained high positions on merit, like Trajan, the future Emperor, who came from Spain, most thoroughly Romanised of all the provinces.

Suetonius pays Vespasian an unusual tribute, saying that no innocent people were punished by him. Yet he faced opposition in the Senate and several conspiracies, and in 71 he banished philosophers and astrologers from Rome. Among the former were the Cynics—the name is derived from the Greek for 'dog'—because of their readiness to snarl. When Demetrius the Cynic continued to attack the Emperor from outside Rome, Vespasian merely remarked: 'I don't kill dogs for barking.'

The philosophers seem to have been allowed to return later, and in 75 the Cynics caused a minor crisis by denouncing a proposed marriage between Titus and Berenice, who had come to Rome with Agrippa. She was ostentatious, exotic and still seductive—a new Cleopatra, perhaps, who had turned another Antony's head. Titus had one of the Cynics flogged, another executed, but in the end he yielded to hostile public opinion, and sent his Jewish princess away. She returned once more in 79, the year Titus became Emperor, but after a short stay withdrew for good—and passes out of history.

The last year of Vespasian's life was a sad one. A plague broke out in Rome, and he discovered a final conspiracy against him. But the man who had always laughed at flatterers kept his sense of humour during a fatal illness, remarking on his death-bed: *'Ut puto, deus fio'* (I think I'm becoming a god). And deified he was, deserving the honour more than most Emperors.

Titus only survived his father by two years: he died of fever in 81. Called 'the darling of mankind', he forgave plotters, punished informers, ordered no executions or treason trials, gave lavish games, and was extremely generous to individuals and cities. Only the Jews went on hating him for the destruction of Jerusalem and the Temple, so brutally commemorated in his Arch at Rome. They saw the eruption of Vesuvius in September 79, which buried the cities of Pompeii and Herculaneum, as a prelude to divine retribution on Titus. There was also a widespread belief that Nero was still alive and well and somewhere in the East: the prophecies said he would cross the Euphrates on his triumphant return, and that the last days would be heralded by a Parthian invasion. A pretender—the famous 'false Nero'—received promises of help from the Parthian king, but got no further because Parthia was in its usual state of internal dissension.

Another disaster occurred in Titus's brief reign: a new fire of Rome, which wiped out several temples, important libraries, and a large part of the whole city. Josephus's house was probably spared, or he would surely have mentioned the damage, especially to his work: he was already deep in his comprehensive history of the Jews, the *Antiquities*. With his imperial subsidy, revenue from his estates, and sales of his first book, he was certainly among the wealthy. Their standards, and the magnificent public buildings, were in striking contrast to the squalid slums in which most of the citizens lived. It was only forty or fifty years later that Hadrian, the great architect Emperor, paid attention to their needs, designing the capital on a sounder basis.

Domitian, who succeeded his brother Titus, must have found much fire damage still unrepaired. He filled libraries with new books, (which no doubt proved useful for Josephus), although it was said that Tiberius's Memoirs and dispatches were all the Emperor ever read. He modelled himself on Tiberius, and like his model paid much attention to maintaining good government in the provinces.

A strange, complex character, very different from his open-handed brother, Domitian was moody, puritanical and aloof, yet a lover of Greece. Rome saw contests in literature, chariot-racing and athletics, at which he presided in Greek dress: the aristocracy disapproved, as they had done in Nero's day. A short campaign in Germany earned him a triumph, he took the title of Germanicus, and the months of September and October were renamed Germanicus and Domitian; after his supression of a revolt in Africa, courtiers greeted him as Master and God. But in 89 a new civil war threatened, when the legions in Upper Germany acclaimed their general as Emperor. The conspiracy was crushed, thanks to a loyal general in Lower Germany, but the experience shattered Domitian's confidence and gradually turned him into the murderous tyrant pictured in later history.

From then on, grim and embittered, he suspected everybody, especially Senators, who were his chief victims. Informers flourished as in the worst days, men of ability retired from public life, Tacitus and other writers remained silent—to get their revenge after his death. At the beginning of 95 a minor poet could present the Emperor as a new sun in the sky. Rome was full of gold and silver statues he had built, and outward show hid the rising tension. Flatterers sacrificed before the Emperor's image until it became normal and expected; any who failed to conform could be charged with atheism. During that year, his cousin Clemens, who looked for a time like the chosen heir, and his niece, Clemens's wife, were executed with others as atheists. Both Jews and Christians claimed them later as sympathisers.

The followers of these religions were by Roman standards the worst and most obstinate of atheists, because it was on principle that they rejected the state's gods as well as Emperor-worship. As a result, both met severe persecution at the end of Domitian's reign, just as each faith was recovering in its own way from the effects of the war.

When news reached Jamnia in 70 that the Temple was burning, the aged Rabbi Johanan, who had established his academy there—he called it 'the Vineyard'—comforted Joshua, his leading disciple, with the words: 'Do not grieve too much, my son, we still possess one means of atonement more effective than sacrifice: acts of loving-kindness.' Corrupt priests, and Zealots preaching hatred, had alike been responsible for the destruction of Jerusalem; the Romans were only God's agents in bringing the proud low. Joshua too, an outstanding and saintly character, saw Judaism as a universal religion in which all lost sheep could be rescued through repentance.

Johanan, Joshua and their colleagues made the vineyard into a new spiritual centre of Judaism. A new Sanhedrin was formed to act as chief tribunal and religious authority for Jews everywhere. But they also made it the responsibility of every Jewish community to see that the correct ritual and ceremonial were observed. This emphasis on local authority started an extraordinary process of decentralisation, which enabled Judaism to survive through the centuries without a religious headquarters or a national home.

The Vineyard rabbis and their successors still treated ethical and social demands as priorities. Their code aimed at preserving family life, protecting the rights of free labour and improving conditions for slaves, correcting social inequalities; above all, it proclaimed peace and human brotherhood as the fundamental principles of religion. Sabbath, synagogue and school testified to these values, and the rabbinic courts of justice developed a sensitivity and compassion not achieved by Christian justice until the nineteenth century, and then only in some countries.

The Vineyards existence was a great stimulus to the Jews who had remained in Judaea. Seven synagogues even in Jerusalem had escaped, and a new generation began to grow up which adapted to the new order as best it could. Sadducees and Essenes disappeared, there were no Zealots as such, and Last-Day fanatics like the Nazarenes were excluded from synagogue worship. They were squeezed out between their fellow Jews, who rejected their Messiah, and other Christians, who wanted to escape from all association with the Jewish faith and ceremonies.

Matthew's Gospel appeared about 80, probably in Alexandria. The Church there claimed a special status because the Holy Family had fled to Egypt, and perhaps because Peter was apostle to the Egyptians—Matthew brings out Peter's primacy: 'Upon this rock I will build my church.' He also quotes: 'All who take the sword shall perish by the sword'—possibly remembering the Nazarenes who had joined their fellow-Jews in the rebellion against Rome. But basically, for him, the whole war was a terrible disaster which had come upon the Jews as a punishment for rejecting the Messiah.

By the time Luke's Gospel came out some years later, the Pauline idea of Christ was accepted almost universally throughout the churches in the Empire. Paul's epistles, written in Greek, were easily available. To eliminate the image of rebelliousness and 'hatred of the human race', the Christians had to show they were a peaceful, moral, law-abiding community. Yet despite the growing hostility between the two faiths, Christianity enjoyed the protection of Judaism for over half a century, and even at the end of

Domitian's reign few people outside had them clearly distinguished.

Thousands of Jews sold as slaves were soon given their freedom—with all their scruples they did not make good slaves: that was one reason why Jews recovered their position in the Empire so quickly. Judaism was still an authorised religion, and converts became entitled to all the Jews' privileges, though they had to pay the two-drachma tax. Those who were born Jews, if they did not attend synagogues, were exempt from this tax—until Domitian started on his policy of 'getting tough' with the atheists. Then informers began denouncing people who tried to hide their Jewish origins, and the tax was collected, says Suetonius, with special ruthlessness.

Domitian was disturbed by oracles prophesying doom on himself and Rome; he evidently felt threatened by 'the Jewish peril'. In 95 he issued a decree expelling all Jews from the Empire within thirty days, on pain of death for any who stayed. The leading Vineyard rabbis hurriedly set off for Rome in the depths of winter to plead for their people. The decree was rescinded, although their arrival coincided with the execution of Clemens.

But by now Domitian's tyranny had reached the stage where no one in high circles felt safe. Eventually the blow fell which he had tried to guard against. They were all in the plot, his wife Domitia, palace officials, Praetorian prefects. A freedman stabbed him to death, but was then quickly killed by loyal guards. The Senate hastily chose Nerva, a mild elderly lawyer, as Emperor. Domitian's acts were abolished, his statues pulled down, political prisoners were released, the persecution of Jews and Christians abruptly stopped. The Senators had a special coin struck celebrating 'the removal of the scandal of the Jewish tax'—which showed an unusual sympathy towards the Jews.

It was all in keeping with Nerva's policy of leniency and relaxation. He swore not to kill any Senator—but the Praetorians mutinied and forced him to execute Domitian's murderers. Another civil war seemed imminent, until Nerva formally adopted as his heir the energetic governor of Upper Germany, Trajan. Three months later Nerva died and Trajan the Spaniard became Emperor, the first man born outside Italy to be nominated. He ruled for twenty years, to be followed by Hadrian, who ruled another twenty-two. The Roman Empire's happiest age had begun, or at least the eighty years which saw least interruptions to prosperity and civil peace.

Did Josephus live to see the better times start? There is another mystery here. We know he completed his *Antiquities* in 93 (he dates it himself), and he presumably wrote his two other works soon afterwards. All three are dedicated to the same patron, Epaphroditus, a literary man from Alexandria who lived in Rome and had a huge library. The last two writings are very short, and one, the *Life*, is an appendix to *Antiquities*, while the other, *Against Apion*, is a reply to criticisms of both his long works as well as a defence of the Jews.

At the end of *Antiquities* he says he wants to publish a new, shorter version of *The Jewish War*, and he might have been writing this when he died, only then some fragments of it would probably have survived. A passage in the *Life* refers to Agrippa as no longer alive, and if Agrippa died in 93, as some scholars think, perhaps Josephus did not survive his friend by many months. This would explain why in the brief piece of real autobiography at the end of the *Life* he does not refer to Nerva or Trajan and still seems proud to have Domitian and his wife as patrons.

Was Josephus still alive when the Vineyard rabbis made their dash to Rome? To help plead their cause, they would surely have been to see 'the most famous Jew of his time', who two years earlier had published the first history of his people in Greek; if they visited him, tradition would have mentioned it. Or had he already fallen from grace, another victim of the Emperor's suspicions? Again, we could expect some note of this by one of his contemporaries. Nor is there any sign in his own work that Domitian's campaign against the atheists was hotting up. Perhaps he died before things got really bad.

Justus of Tiberias had accused Josephus of anti-Roman activities in the war, and in the *Life* Josephus turns the tables by demonstrating that Justus himself played a discreditable part and asking why he only produced his history *now*, when many of the people involved (like Agrippa), who could have confirmed or refuted it, were already dead; also, Justus was quite unqualified to know the facts about Josephus in Galilee. But Justus was a Jew, and Josephus refers to his *Jewish* accusers punished by Domitian, with never a hint that he was under pressure from the Roman side or felt threatened by informers.

Nor did he show any defensiveness about publishing *Antiquities*, 'in the belief that the whole Greek-speaking world will find it worthy of attention; for it will take in our entire ancient history and political constitution, translated from the Hebrew records'. A century earlier Dionysus of Halicarnassus had published an 'Ancient History of the Romans' in twenty books, and here was Josephus boldly offering the same *magnum opus* on the Jews—also in twenty books.

It falls into four parts. The first and longest, from the Creation to the end of the Old Testament period, is largely a rewriting of the Bible with some omissions and some changes or additions from secular authorities. Despite claims to the contrary, Josephus clearly 'improved on' the Biblical narrative at times or used his imagination for the sake of a good story. In the second part (up to 145 B.C.) he could draw on Greek and Roman writers, notably the Greek historian Polybius (204—122 B.C.). Polybius had also been a prisoner of the Romans and was also kindly treated by a Roman patron—the last of the three great Scipios. Like Josephus, he served his defeated nation by glorifying Rome and interpreting Rome's victory over his native land as the work of providence or destiny.

The third part runs to the accession of Archelaus (4 B.C.), for which the works of Nicolaus of Damascus, Herod's court historian, were Josephus's most important source; and the last part from then till the outbreak of war in 66, the period for which full and reliable details would be specially interesting. But these last three books, unfortunately, are the least satisfactory, partly because documentary evidence was hard to obtain, partly because his research assistant for this period was less competent than earlier 'ghosts' had been.

He had many more sources to investigate for *Antiquities* than for *The Jewish War*, and so used his 'ghosts' more extensively. On the whole they served him well. We can't tell how much he wrote himself and how much he left to them, though sometimes their work seems to be brought in only half digested. *Antiquities* lacks the dramatic unity and climax of *The Jewish War*, and is not nearly so gripping or well-constructed. With some quite irrelevant sections, it is often either long-winded or disjointed and scrappy. Yet considering all the difficulties he faced in such an ambitious project, Josephus achieved a good deal of his aims.

Throughout the work he stresses that God is active in human history and specially concerned with His chosen people: here is the historian's ultimate justification for writing their history. From *The Jewish War* readers might take away the impression of a brave but barbarous and fanatical nation. *Antiquities* tries to restore the balance by showing a people of high moral standards, resolutely obeying their ancient and sacred traditions.

He aims more directly at this in *Against Apion*, a calm, balanced pamphlet refuting Greek 'antisemitism'—courageous too, if Domitian, lover of Greece, was still alive. It claims Moses as the greatest and oldest of law-givers, and defends the antiquity of Jewish civilization, based on more accurate and authentic traditions than those of the Greeks. More generally, it refutes the ignorant prejudices against Jews which were common even among the educated classes at Rome.

Even Tacitus, for instance, asserts that the Jews worshipped an ass; this was one of the libels Josephus nailed. He also wanted to wipe out the anti-Gentile image with examples of Jewish tolerance and benevolence: 'Those who wish to come under our laws are given a friendly welcome.' All men, even foes, are to be treated 'gently and humanely'. People everywhere are attracted by 'our harmonious living with each other, the charitable distribution of our goods, our hard work in the crafts, and our courage in persecution on behalf of our laws'.

Jews are not bigoted or hostile to their fellows even on religion: 'Our laws have expressly forbidden us to deride or blaspheme the gods recognised by others, out of respect for the very word God.' They also submit readily to defeat

169

except when pressure is put on them to alter their statutes; but it is an instinct with every Jew 'to regard the Scriptures as the decrees of God, to abide by them, and if need be, cheerfully to die for them ... What Greek would endure as much for the same cause? Even to save the entire collection of his nation's writings from destruction he would not face the smallest personal injury.'

Josephus often uses superficial arguments, for most of his Greek readers were not deep thinkers. But sometimes he brings flashes of insight which shine forth brightly in noble tributes to his people—like this observation in *Against Apion*: 'The greatest miracle of all is that our Law holds out no bait of sensual pleasure, but has exercised this influence through its own inherent merits; and as God permeates the universe, so the Law has found its way among all mankind.'

Coin of Domitian

EPILOGUE:
THE THINGS THAT
ARE CAESAR'S

We do not know what happened to Josephus's sons. If they lived their allotted span and remained in any sense Jews, they had occasion to experience their father's conflict of loyalties during two further Jewish rebellions against Rome.

The first occurred outside Judaea in 115 and 116, while Trajan was campaigning in Parthia. Once he and his army had crossed the Euphrates, the Jews of Babylon rose behind it. At the same time, perhaps in concert with them, the Jews of Cyrene, Egypt and Cyprus also broke out in revolt, slaughtering thousands of their fellow-citizens. In Cyrene another 'Messiah' prepared for a 'return to Zion'. Cyrene, Alexandria and other cities were wrecked, and the rebels too suffered very heavy casualties. It took three years before they were conquered and peace restored.

Under Hadrian, a benevolent despot specially concerned with good government in the Empire, things at first looked better. He had Trajan's statue removed from the 'Holy Mountain' (site of the Temple), his nephew Aquilas was converted to Judaism, and the leading rabbis—who had moved their headquarters from Jamnia to Galilee—understood that he was to rebuild Jerusalem. They even hoped for permission to rebuild the Temple. Whatever Hadrian's earlier intentions, the fine new city he eventually decided on was not for the Jews: he made designs for a Gentile city, to be called Aelia Capitolina, which would assert Roman supremacy against a new rising tide of Jewish nationalism. He also banned circumcision, a decree his successor was to revoke.

The rabbis disagreed on how to react to these attacks on the faith, but patriotic fervour won the day. After sixty years' servitude, a longer period than the captivity in Babylon, the Jews must now strike a blow once more for freedom. A new Messiah appeared, Simon Bar Kochba ('Son of the Star'), and was hailed as such by the venerable Rabbi Akiba—who was finally to be martyred by the Romans. In 132, as the first buildings of Aelia Capitolina were going up, Bar Kochba launched his revolt, and at first gained a series of victories over local Roman forces. Coins were struck with 'Jerusalem' on one side, 'Year 1 of the Redemption of Israel' on the other. He was bitterly anti-Christian, for the Christians recognised a different Messiah, and the break between Christians and Jews now became complete. Fighting with fanatical courage, the rebels were gradually driven into a single fortress south-west of Jerusalem, Bethara, where they held out successfully for two years.

Hadrian had to bring Severus, his ablest general, from Britain, before the Romans at last captured and destroyed the fortress. In the three and a half years of war hundreds of thousands of Jews died, and the suffering and destruction were if anything greater than two generations before. The names Judaea and Jerusalem were expunged from the Roman language. Judaea became Palestina, while Hadrian's model city of Aelia Capitolina was built to the design which in general lay-out Jerusalem still has today. For some time Jews were only allowed to visit it once a year. Most of the Jewish population which remained in Palestine now lived in Galilee, but many thousands of Jews had fled during the war to Babylon, outside the Empire's bounds.

Babylon and Alexandria became the most important centres of Judaism, and from there the Jews spread out into Arabia, southern Europe and along the north coast of Africa. But the Romans made the descendants of Hillel 'patriarchs', and the Jewish patriarchate remained in existence at Tiberias until the 5th century. A small community of Jews even grew up in and around Aelia Capitolina. There has always, in fact, been a Jewish community living at Jerusalem, save for a period after Jews had been massacred by the Crusaders. It was not till the nineteenth century, however, that the city could claim the largest Jewish population in Palestine: 5,000 in 1844 (to 6,000 Moslems and 4,000 Christians), 30,000 at the end of the century (to 11,000 Christians, 7,000 Moslems). Most of the Jewish inhabitants were pious and orthodox, who had returned to the holiest of their holy cities. The blessing Jews said after meals ran: 'Have mercy, O Lord, upon Israel thy people, upon Jerusalem thy city.'

After Bar Kochba the Jews gave Rome no further trouble as a nation, while they continued to survive as a people scattered over the Empire. They were still sustained by their unshakable belief in a loving and almighty God, plus a combination of high ideals and ritual observances—'complicated, archaic and cumbersome', as one critic has called them—relating to every part of daily life.

The Christians, without the burden of such rituals, had an equally strong inducement to personal morality in the teachings and example of their Saviour, who had inspired so many thousands of martyrs. Roman persecution varied in intensity, sometimes lapsing into mere official disapproval. The Christians survived it, to make vast numbers of converts and finally get their faith recognised as the state religion by the Emperor Constantine at the beginning of the fourth century. The state won the real victory. Now 'established', the Church became even more absorbed in savage theological battles and heresy hunts, which took it further than ever from the ideals of love, compassion and humility proclaimed by Jesus of Nazareth.

Eusebius, Bishop of Caesarea under Constantine, and father of Church history, quotes Josephus often, and speaks of the high esteem in which both Jews and Romans held him. Another historian of the early Church calls him 'the Greek Livy'. Pagan writers also showed an interest in him; early translations into Latin spread knowledge of the man and his works. Christians treasured these works as a source of vital background information on affairs in Palestine during New Testament times. Ironically, the Church venerated this Jew, turned defender of the Roman Empire, above all for the passages referring to John the Baptist, Jesus and James. Their genuineness was then taken for 'gospel'.

The first English translation of Josephus was made in 1640, but a later one by Rev. William Whiston, published in 1737, became the standard English version; and many homes, if they owned no other books, would have their copy of Whiston with the family Bible. Till quite recent times, familiarity with Josephus was evidently spread over a wide area of British society: in Kipling's *Captains Courageous* a seaman recited on Sunday from an old leather-bound volume of Josephus, 'very solid and very like a

Bible, but enlivened with accounts of battles and sieges'.

For centuries his reputation as a historian was equally solid. But modern scholars gradually came to realise that his reliability had been taken too much for granted. For most of *The Jewish War* there were no extant works by other authorities of the time against which to check his facts and the way he presented them. When Josephus the man was reassessed, it also threw doubts on his truthfulness: with his immense vanity and so many personal axes to grind, he could scarcely be trusted on any important issue.

Probably the reaction went too far. Other historians have allowed their own prejudices too much play, omitting inconvenient facts, whitewashing their heroes and blackening their villains. Josephus was specially exposed to these temptations because he was so heavily involved in the events he described. But he could still pay tribute to the Zealots' courage, recording faithfully their arguments and actions at Masada, which stood in such contrast to his own in the cave.

For Masada his accuracy has been confirmed, and the same applies to those of his geographical descriptions which can be checked today. He provides, too, a wealth of detail on the life of the times which he knew from his own experience and passed on to his readers without any propaganda purpose. He captures very convincingly the atmosphere of the 'Jewish War' with its horror, brutality and occasional heroism. On the whole, he told an exciting story carefully and conscientiously, putting all he knew into it, and when we come to a period beyond his writings, as the historian Stewart Perowne says, 'our loss is like crossing the line between the sown and the desert'.

As for Josephus's faults of character, his complacency, treachery and low cunning, he was often his own worst enemy in exposing these faults to the public gaze—apparently without intending it. This at least goes for his brief period as a man of action; on other periods the record is too incomplete to judge him. His first visit to Rome, pleading for the imprisoned priests, was after all a creditable one, and for his later life—the tone of *Antiquities* is distinctly less pro-Roman. Perhaps he became increasingly disenchanted with Roman society, and appreciated all the more his Jewish heritage.

What did it mean to be a Jew living in Rome? Then as today, citizenship of one country, and attachment to a quite different cultural tradition based on a religion, made it very hard for a Jew to decide just where he 'belonged'. The confusion was increased for Josephus with the start of a new chapter: national independence utterly lost. But the community of Jews spread all over the Roman Empire could still be seen as the guardian of great ideals, representing the Torah, God's eternal Law, which penetrated every area of Jewish life. The Torah must stop the Jew from sinking into the broad mass of heathen culture.

Devout Jews in that age feared assimilation as much as many Jews still do today: with better reason, for of course the difference of standards between Jew and Gentile was far greater than it is now. True, many thousands were still encouraged and uplifted by the mystery religions, and there was nobility in the old philosophies derived from Greece. But most ordinary people in the Empire did not live on the high level of Stoics or Epicureans; life for them was what the famous English philosopher, Thomas Hobbes, called it— 'solitary, poor, nasty, brutish and short'. The ancient gods of Greece and Rome gave them little comfort or inspiration to rise above such an environment.

The Jew might still sink into it. We hear of all the

converts, but little of the thousands of Jews who must have given up the struggle to live differently from their neighbours. They were the more tempted because of the basic tolerance in the Graeco-Roman attitude to religion, which assumed that different peoples were worshipping the same gods under different names, and that there was no harm in mixing up their names, ideas and identities.

Strict Jewish tradition could not unbend to accept this attitude. Josephus tried to come to terms with it, and succeeded better than most: what he gave away in compromise, he made up for by his ability to live peacefully in a Gentile society. Was it possible to remain a good Jew in such a society? Josephus thought it was. He did not renounce his faith, as did his contemporary, Tiberius Alexander, who also rose high in the Gentile world.

The story of Josephus raises a final important question in the area where politics, morals and religion meet. The Roman Empire provided a rule of law with at least a principle of impartial justice. Its roads, communications and currency gave a secure basis for international trade and travel which benefited all the subject peoples, including the Jews. Caesar's image on the coins symbolised real blessings which were easier to appreciate when they vanished, as in times of civil war.

Yet Roman rule was achieved and maintained by curbing national aspirations. Aldous Huxley once called the patience of the oppressed the most inexplicable fact in all history. In Roman history it was an almost universal fact, but it is strange that in this century Huxley could find it hard to explain. Faced by all the power of the modern state, how can the oppressed rise against their oppressors with any hope of success? But rise they still do from time to time, for the human spirit is unconquerable—usually, however, with tragic results.

Through the centuries the Jews in particular have had little chance of even a token rising; the hopeless struggle of the Warsaw Ghetto was an extraordinary exception. That is why many Jews today admire so much the military prowess shown by the modern state of Israel, sometimes forgetting that the Jewish mission is essentially to help bring about peace and brotherhood for all mankind. This was the reason why God chose the Jews as His people: they were not to think themselves superior to other peoples; their only privilege was to have a greater responsibility.

The late Levi Eshkol, former Prime Minister of Israel, claimed that for nearly two thousand years the Jews have always yearned for peace, and that through all ordeals 'they placed their trust in the biblical promise that they would one day return to Israel and there at last find peace'. He was surely right in his claim.

But when they returned and proclaimed the new Israel in 1948, when they 'came home' to the whole of Jerusalem in the triumphant days of June 1967, the glory of the home-coming showed an ugly stain: it meant injustice to many of the people who were then living in the Jews' promised land. Dispossessed for so long, the Jews were now dispossessing others.

The ancient Israelites, on reaching Canaan, had gradually conquered all their neighbours. In the twentieth century the people of Israel could never do that, even if they wanted to. They have to go on living among the other peoples of the Middle East, almost all of whom are at present hostile. Even if territory has to be given up, Israel *must* have peace for long-term survival. The other side of the coin, of course, is that peace is equally important for the Arab world, even if it means that the state of Israel—born, as they see it, in injustice—has to be accepted as a permanent feature on the Middle Eastern map.

The Arab world has not yet accepted this, and would like, if possible, to wipe that feature out. So how far should the Jews make sacrifices, even of national independence, for the sake of an insecure peace? It was the same agonising problem, though in a different form, which racked the Jews of Josephus's age.

The Roman occupation of Judaea was just as intolerable as many modern occupations have been. Josephus, born rich and an aristocrat, was spared a good deal of its hardships. But he saw just as clearly the greed, scorn and corruption of most of the procurators and their Syrian officials, and the legions' hatred. Only, he went to Rome as a young man and understood its power: why fight a hopeless war when better days might come? It was no good expecting divine aid. Even if the Jews had not already forfeited this by their sins and impiety, they had before now faced defeat, subjection and captivity, without God deserting them.

Most people's motives are mixed most of the time, and Josephus followed his instinct for self-preservation, while genuinely believing as a matter of policy that peace at any price might be the lesser of two evils. He was no saint or martyr, and could never have followed the ideal of non-violent resistance to evil which we associate with Jesus of Nazareth or in modern times with Gandhi and Martin Luther King. But he realised that violence bred more violence, that guerilla attacks led to still harsher repression, that patriotism was very far from enough.

As a result future generations of Jews have hated him as what we now call a 'Quisling', who collaborated with the enemy rather than fighting to the bitter end. But after basely saving his life and achieving security, this friend, protégé and servant of Caesar fought for his people after his own fashion, acknowledging their age-old covenant with God and revealing it to the Gentiles, writing their history so as to put them in the best possible light with their conquerors and the world, defending them against their enemies with courage, skill and conviction—to the end of his days. To that extent Flavius Josephus, formerly Joseph Ben Matthias, rendered unto God the things that are God's, and surely, in the calm light of history, redeemed his honour as a good Jew.

Coin of Vespasian (A.D. 69) inscribed JUDAEA CAPTA. 'SC' *stands for Senatus Consultu (by Order of the Senate). The figure on the left represents a Roman general holding in his left hand the 'palladium' emblem of Pallas Athene, goddess of victory. At the foot of the palm tree sits a grieving woman, symbolic of conquered Judaea*

Suggestions
for Further Reading

Selections from Josephus's works
JOSEPHUS, The Jewish War and other Selections from
  Flavius Josephus, edited and abridged with an Introduc-
  tion by Moses I. Finlay. New English Library (paper-
  back), 1966.
JERUSALEM AND ROME, the Writings of Josephus, selected
  and introduced by Nahum N. Glatzer. Fontana (paper-
  back), 1966.
THE JEWISH WAR, (transl. G. A. Williamson), Penguin
  Classics.

Other Authors
Moses Aberbach: THE ROMAN–JEWISH WAR 66–70 A.D.,
  Jewish Quarterly, 1966.
S. G. F. Brandon: THE FALL OF JERUSALEM AND THE
  CHRISTIAN CHURCH, Society for Promoting Christian
  Knowledge, 1951.
  JESUS AND THE ZEALOTS, Manchester University
  Press, 1965.
  THE TRIAL OF JESUS OF NAZARETH, Batsford, 1968;
  Paladin (paper-back), 1971.
W. R. Farmer: MACCABEES, ZEALOTS AND JOSEPHUS,
  Oxford University Press, 1957.
A. H. M. Jones: THE HERODS OF JUDAEA, Oxford Univer-
  sity Press, 1938.

James Parkes: HISTORY OF THE JEWISH PEOPLE, Pelican, 1964.
Stewart Perowne: THE LIFE AND TIMES OF HEROD THE GREAT; THE LATER HERODS, both Hodder & Stoughton, 1956.
Hugh Schonfield: THE PASSOVER PLOT, Hutchinson, 1965. THOSE INCREDIBLE CHRISTIANS, Hutchinson, 1968.
H. St. J. Thackeray: JOSEPHUS THE MAN AND HISTORIAN, New York, 1929.
G. A. Williamson: THE WORLD OF JOSEPHUS, Secker and Warburg, 1964.
Edmund Wilson: THE DEAD SEA SCROLLS 1947–1969, W. H. Allen, 1969.
Yigael Yadin: MASADA, Weidenfeld and Nicolson, 1966.

Index

184

JE

☐Family
Tomb of
Herod

HINNOM VALLEY

THE UPPER

Herod's
Palace

Tower
of
David

Aqueduct

First w

THE LOWER CITY

TYROPOEON

VALLEY

Ou
Co

T

W

S + N

E

KIDRO